Looking Back

Memoirs of a World War II Combat Medic

Ronald E. Coe, MD

104th Timberwolf Infantry

Division K Company 414th

Regiment, Medic

iUniverse, Inc.
New York   Bloomington

Looking Back
Memoirs of a World War II Combat Medic

Photos are courtesy of Ronald E. Coe, MD unless otherwise noted in the photo caption.

Cover photo and the final photo of the book are self-portraits taken by Ron Coe of he and his wife, Eleanor on top of the Lake Placid Ski Jump (Lake Placid, New York) in 1944.

iUniverse books may be ordered through booksellers or by contacting:

iUniverse
1663 Liberty Drive
Bloomington, IN 47403
www.iuniverse.com
1-800-Authors (1-800-288-4677)

Because of the dynamic nature of the Internet, any Web addresses or links contained in this book may have changed since publication and may no longer be valid.

ISBN: 978-1-4502-2019-4 (sc)
ISBN: 978-1-4502-2021-7 (dj)
ISBN: 978-1-4502-2020- 0 (ebk)

Printed in the United States of America

iUniverse rev. date: 7/7/2010

This book is dedicated to my wife, Eleanor, who has been my pal since our early teenage years. She has been my partner and in her own way endured the war effort back home in the United States. Eleanor spotted airplanes in U.S. airspace while sitting shifts in area lookout towers. I have been blessed to share my life and love with Eleanor and to have her lifelong support.

"I have been tired, wet, and cold, but always I thought of your love, and I was comforted...."
(Excerpt from a letter from Ron to Eleanor written during the war)

Disclaimer

These stories are accurate to the best of my recollection. Some names have been changed to protect the privacy of my fellow comrades.

Contents

Acknowledgments

When I started to write this book, I thought it was just a matter of jotting down a few notes. I quickly learned that one person does not do this alone. I owe my daughter, Nancy, a great deal of thanks for transcribing my stories and making many edits. Without her, this book would not be possible. I would also like to thank Anita Oliva, a friend and patient as well as a writer and editor, for her edits, confidence, and honesty; Jane Marshall, a friend and neighbor who is a seasoned English teacher, for graciously making additional edits; and my grandson, Josh, who at the time of this writing is eerily the exact age that I was when I left for war, for making additional contextual and grammatical edits. I am grateful to all these folks for caring about my desire to share these stories and for helping me to do so.

Introduction

This book is essentially a recollection of my experiences as a combat medic with the 104th Infantry Division during World War II. At the start of the war, I was a premed student at Colby College in Waterville, Maine. I joined the Army Reserve in order to complete the current semester of college rather than wait for the draft. The Army Reserve guaranteed a college student the time to complete the current semester of college, while the draft came with no such guarantee. The reality of being a soldier in war was still surreal to me. When the time came to begin active service on June 8, 1943, I was proud to serve.

My desire in writing this book was not to tell the gory details of war but to tell the emotional and human side of war. These pages could easily be filled with bloody stories of mangled bodies and vivid depictions of the war that are a part of every medic's daily life. While these vivid details remain etched in my memory, to what avail would these horrid memories be today for the reader or for the legacy of those whose lives were taken by war? Rather, it is the emotional and human side of war that I wish to preserve. This war was filled with human beings who had lives outside the war and families whom they loved dearly. Furthermore, as a medic, it never mattered to me which uniform these soldiers wore; they were young men just like me.

It is my hope that these stories evoke emotions such that you, the reader, cannot help but be touched by the humanistic side of this war. It is the individual and the ethos of each life that is permanently imprinted in my personal being. These soldiers, whose lives were taken at such young ages and by such cruel and unfair circumstances, were, despite their nationalities, all human beings. They were young men whose lives and potential before the war were not much different than mine. I hope that through reading the stories of these brave young individuals, you can begin to understand how cruel and unfair war is.

Timberwolves referred to the soldiers belonging to the 104th Infantry Division, a division that began at the end of World War I. The division was originally made up of soldiers from the western part of the United States and was at that time called the Frontier Division. During World War II, the Frontier Division became the Timberwolf Division and had soldier representation from all areas of the United States.

After my initial induction into the army, I was enrolled in the ASTP (Army Specialized Training Program). While in the ASTP, my basic training took place at Fort Benning, Georgia. Following basic training, I was sent to Princeton University to study until the army needed more soldiers in combat. When more soldiers were needed, the ASTP was closed and a large influx of college students from all over the country was sent to the Timberwolf Division. On March 15, 1943, I became one of those college students. I joined the Timberwolves at Camp Carson in Colorado Springs, Colorado.

The Princeton Group at Henry Hall

The men originally assigned to the Timberwolf Division had done their basic training at Camp Adair in the Willamette Valley, Oregon. I heard some of the soldiers who trained at Camp Adair say that their training had been physically tougher than actual combat. This is probably true. Those of us who joined the Timberwolves after they had moved to Camp Carson were given additional training, which included specialized training in night fighting to make us fully trained Timberwolves. Fortunately, we mixed in well with the original troops. I once heard it said that soldiers from the ASTP were an asset to the Timberwolf Division. I hope so.

All the soldiers of the 104th Infantry Division (Timberwolves) served under Commanding Officer Major General Terry De La Mesa Allen. We wore the division patch showing a western gray Timberwolf against a green background and the motto "Nothing in hell can stop the Timberwolves." Major General Terry De La Mesa Allen was a West Pointer who served in World War I and World War II. He was well respected by the troops, not only for serving in two wars but also for being a fine leader and human being. The respect between the soldiers and their leader was mutual. Under his command, our morale remained high, and I never witnessed any significant disagreement among the troops. We liked him and willingly followed his orders. In World War II, he headed two divisions with outstanding combat records, namely the First Division, known as The Big Red One, and our division, the 104th Infantry Division, known as the Timberwolves. I am proud to be one of the many who served under him.

The pages that follow recall much of my exposure as a combat medic with the 104th Infantry Division, 414th Regiment, Company K. Our platoon started combat in Holland and Belgium on October 23, 1944, and remained in that area until November 8, 1944. We then moved into Germany until the war ended on May 7, 1945. We endured 195 days of continuous combat throughout Holland, Belgium, and Germany. Throughout these stories, I make some references to actual combat injuries, but for the most part, the injury details have been left out. It does not take much imagination to visualize what explosive devices and automatic weapons can do to the human body. These injuries and the horrifying details will remain forever in my memory bank. Simply stated, war is horrible and inhumane.

The memories and friendships that I made during the war have lasted a lifetime. Those who died during the war and those who lived to an old age and died of natural causes leave a similar void and deep pain of loss. Our numbers are now dwindling as those of us who survived the war take the last bugle call.

Ronald E. Coe, MD
Hamden, Connecticut
June 2009

*104ᵗʰ Infantry Division
Timberwolf Patch*

A Slow Adjustment to War

Durham Public Library

My initial contact with the realities of combat unfolded in the safe confines of the basement of the Durham Public Library in Durham, Connecticut. I was in high school in 1938 when on a rainy Saturday afternoon, I opened a soft, brown, leather-bound book titled *The Horror of It ... Camera Records of War's Gruesome Glories* by Frederick A. Barber. The book was filled with exceedingly graphic pictures of wounded and dead gassed victims from World War I. These pictures left me with a strange and sickening feeling, but even stranger was my feeling of remoteness from World War II.

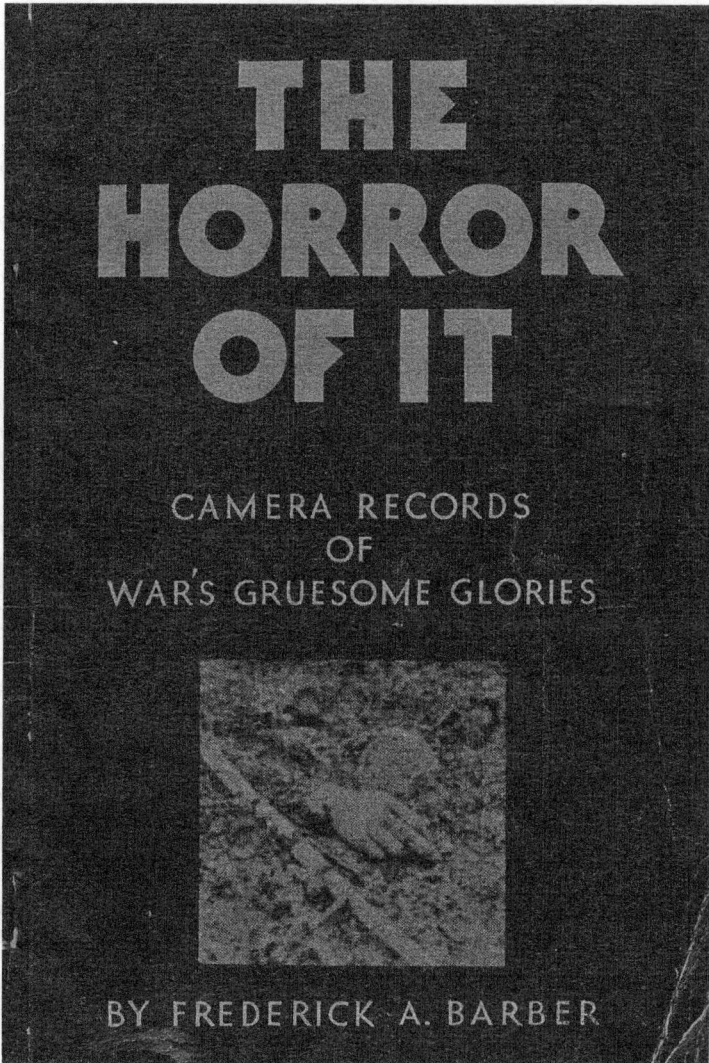

As time passed, the increasing number of military convoys passing through the little town of Durham offered mounting evidence of the impending war, but still I had not embraced the realities of war. After high school, I went on to Colby College in Waterville, Maine, as a premed student. Watching the U.S. Army Air Force students march in formation to their classes as a college student, I cannot recall ever thinking of myself as a combatant. Even after joining the Army Reserve in Portland, Maine, during the middle of my sophomore year, I did not face the obvious reality of the near future. I joined the Army Reserve so that I would be permitted to finish the current semester of college. It seemed a better alternative to the draft, but the consequences of this action had not yet hit home.

In June 1943, after completing my sophomore year of college, I reported to Fort Devens in Massachusetts and began my journey through several camps, including Fort Benning in Georgia, for basic infantry training. Although this training included experience with many different weapons, I could not imagine using one to kill another human. I feared taking a life, and by volunteering to be a medic, I was confident that I could avoid killing.

After training in the ASTP at Fort Benning, our group was sent to Princeton, New Jersey, where we were allowed to take academic courses at Princeton University. Finally, we were sent to Camp Carson in Colorado Springs, where we joined the 104th Timberwolf Division. Following five more months of training at the end of August 1944, we were sent to New York City for deployment overseas.

After arriving overseas in 1944, my friend and fellow medic Nils Isachen and I experienced our first combat exposure, and the reality of war finally hit home. It was on the flat, wet soil of Holland that fear and the realities of war took hold with a vengeance. Our senses were immediately awakened to the sights, the sounds, the tastes, the feel, and the smells of war. What took an instant to become real would take a lifetime to process. Decades later, I now know that these realities will stay with me until the day I die. While the reality of war is inescapable, one never fully adjusts. The memories are difficult, if not impossible, to erase.

Fear is a great catalyst in learning survival skills. The first priority was to learn the difference between incoming and outgoing mail—the military terminology for shells and bombs. I have heard it said that you don't hear the one that hits you. I doubt if this is always true. I recall being hit by a shell fragment; I heard the whistle of the fragment, but I didn't hear the shell explosion. One problem is that during heavy shelling, it is impossible to distinguish between the varied and numerous sounds. I do recall in later battles hearing the sounds of bullets whining overhead. I specifically remember climbing the face of Hill 287 in Stolberg, Germany, with my friend Sammy and hearing this sound. The Germans had added another sadistic twist to mortars, which we called "screaming meemies." The "fins" were altered to create a screeching noise, which only added to the horror of being shelled. We would come to know this distinct sound well as we tried to adjust to the daily life of war.

World War II— On Our Way

After the ASTP ended, we were sent to Camp Carson in Colorado to join the 104th Timberwolf Division, which was getting ready to leave for combat. After some five weeks of training, we left Camp Carson by train between August 15 and 17, 1944, and arrived at Camp Kilmer in New Jersey on August 20. We were processed for overseas shipment, which included a final clothing and weapons check for each individual. We also got our last taste of civilized life before shipping out. Prior to shipping out, we had the pleasure of seeing a USO show in which Marlene Dietrich, the German-born actress, performed. In my opinion, the fact that she performed for U.S. troops made her a great and humble lady.

On August 24, 1944, the chaplains gave their final blessings for the men of the 104th, and on August 25 and 26, the division was taken to New York Harbor via coaches, where we boarded ferryboats that shuttled us to our ship, the *USS George Washington*. We walked up the gangplank and entered the ship that would take us to Europe to face the realities of war.

The *USS George Washington* was originally taken from the Germans during World War I. In fact, my father-in-law came back from that war on this vessel. Now, twenty-some years later, another generation was heading to Europe on the same German vessel. It seemed ironic that the same vessel that carried my father-in-law to the safety of home was now carrying my generation to imminent danger. In the darkness, as we passed the Statue of Liberty, I looked up at her, saluted, and whispered, "Good-bye, old lady, I will probably never see you again."

It was a long, slow boat trip. However, my prankster friends helped break the boredom to some degree. My friend Harry Goldberg, who was in the bunk above me, was on the heavy side. We slept on hanging bunks made of canvas material. There were eyelets around the canvas border, with a continuous running line that was tied to a pipe frame to secure the bunks. One night while I was sound asleep, Harry came crashing down on top of me. Our friends had cut him down by severing the line in several places. A rumor ensued that there would be a possible court martial because the soldiers had destroyed government property, but I never heard of that materializing.

Harry Goldberg at The Garden of Gods—
Colorado Springs, Colorado

Another prank involved waiting until a group of soldiers fell sound asleep and then rattling our mess kits and watching as the sleeping soldiers awoke, jumped from their bunks, and walked toward the mess hall after only a short sleep. Laughter helped pass the time.

A small group of us decided that it would be both practical and a good way to pass the time onboard the ship to completely shave our heads in preparation for war. This did not set well with the high-ranking officers, and we were set aside as an example of what not to do. In the military, all must look alike.

We were perhaps one or two days from our landing at Cherbourg, France, when suddenly there was a loud explosion and shaking of the vessel, which was followed by the Navy firing machine guns at the airborne balloon targets. Suddenly, isolated by ourselves, we watched the escort vessels doing what appeared to be excessive maneuvering. Years later I saw an article in the *Timberwolf Howl* (the division's newspaper) explaining what really happened. A German submarine message had been intercepted, and it stated that the *USS George Washington* had been sunk with all troops aboard. Our ship was then moved to a separate location by itself making it appear that we were missing in the formation and thus looking as if we had in fact been sunk. I often wonder if anyone would have jumped overboard had we known the contents of that German message in fear that we could be sunk if the Germans located us out of formation.

We landed at Cherbourg on September 7, 1944. We were the first American division to land directly in France. It was a gloomy, overcast, and rainy day. I recall a crane was unloading the officers' footlockers when the netting or a rope broke, and the lockers tumbled into the water. This was followed by a loud applause, laughter, and cheering from the troops taking advantage of yet another comic relief opportunity.

I was fascinated by the railroad track, which in peacetime would carry passengers right to the water's edge to board their ships. It was here that I saw the first outdoor European bathroom facility and was fascinated by a French couple standing there holding hands. He was inside the latrine, obviously urinating, and she was standing on the outside. I had always heard there were many differences in the European culture compared with ours, and I was now seeing examples of this firsthand.

When we entered the towns of Caen and Saint Lo, France, they appeared to be totally destroyed. The destruction gave us an idea of the explosive powers of war. We then moved into a small village called Valognes, near Barneville, France, where it rained for several days. We pitched our pup tents in an apple orchard. Each soldier carried half a pup tent in his backpack, and we would normally share a tent with one other soldier; however, in this case, we actually put two tents together so that there would be four men to a larger tent—two men on each end. The tents were pitched properly to promote drainage. We went one step further. We found some two-by-six lumber and made a base of this wood around the perimeter, placing three boards on top of each other and then pitching the tents on top of the boards. The orders from the officers in charge were that everything had to be uniform, allowing for the base to be two boards high. Many of us got around this by placing the first board at ground level and covering it on the outside with dirt so that from the outside only two boards were showing, but we still gained an additional six inches of height inside the tent. We also found some fresh straw in barns and electric wire and bulbs from the bombed buildings and French homes. We tapped into the aid station's electric generator and ran the wire underground to our tents, which allowed us light inside our tents. During the day, we buried the interior wires and bulbs in the straw. We never were caught.

Truckers from our division ran what was called the Red Ball Express, which served to supply the front-line troops, especially the tanks, with gasoline and all the other necessities of war. The rest of us passed time by cleaning up fallen apples from the French orchards. We were so cozy and comfortable that we hoped we could spend the duration of the war in Valognes; however, we were realistic and knew that this would not be the case. I recall gazing out at the German-occupied Jersey Islands, which were about ten miles off the shore. Knowing these islands were occupied forced us to face the fact that the war was getting closer.

The day came when we finally had to leave the comfort of our tents. On October 10, 1944, we left the vicinity of Valognes and marched some thirty miles to the English Channel. We could actually see the German soldiers and their camps on the Jersey Islands. The distance between the war and us was now growing closer by the minute.

Comrades L to R: Israel Jaffe, Lee Grille, John Kekich, and Ted Boriskie

On October 15, 1944, we moved out with most of the troops going by rail in the 40 and 8's, (which stands for rail cars used to carry forty men or eight horses), while a few rode in motor vehicles. I was allowed to ride in a Jeep because I was suffering from spontaneous acute tendinitis and tenosynovitis of the Achilles tendon, an inflammation of the tendon and the lining of the tendon sheath respectively, most likely from repetitive marching and walking. That night the rain fell hard, and I found that sleeping in a Jeep all night was not very comfortable. We reached the area of Vilvoorde, Belgium, just north of Brussels on October 20, 1944. While traveling, we passed an area where remnants of World War I were visible because of the elongated snakelike depressions in the ground left over from the old trenches. This gave one a very eerie feeling. We somehow felt luckier than those who had come before us and fought in World War I, because unlike those who fought in that war, we knew the type of warfare we were going to encounter. We knew that this would be a very different war than the one that World War I soldiers had experienced, and we hoped that it would not include poisonous gas attacks as most of us had already thrown the bulky gas masks away. Even in war, decisions and choices are relative.

9

Medic Ron Coe

Hard Cider

After we landed in Normandy, France, we spent about a week waiting to be deployed. Our medical battalion was given passwords and orders for guard duty. Hedgerows rather than fences divided the areas of Normandy. We were to guard the openings in the hedgerows. We were appalled at these orders because we had nothing to defend ourselves with. I remember nervously joking that we couldn't defend ourselves with morphine syrettes.

Our natural response was subtle rebellion. We spent several days visiting French homes and trying to obtain wine. The French homeowners told us that the Germans had taken it all and that they had only hard cider and calvados, a highly alcoholic French apple brandy. We filled our canteens with the hard cider and brandy and drank freely of it. I noticed that some good old Texas boys were showing signs of the effects, but it didn't seem to bother me initially. However, I can honestly say that when it hit, I was truly intoxicated. This is the only time in my life that I experienced such intoxication. I can remember stomping freely all over the shoulders of the roads that had signs warning of mines. I negotiated my way over and around stepping-stones through a swampy section. I am sure the old Texas boys were watching me as I negotiated my path across the stones. They certainly expected that I would fall flat on my face in the water.

Although we spent the night in drunken debauchery, we still had to monitor our guard post. However, rather than taking our shifts in the proper fashion, we guarded from inside our pup tents. When our shifts were over, we would run to the next tent and wake up the next soldier to relieve us of duty. We figured that there were no Germans around and that if a German did stumble by we didn't want to be standing in the middle of the road unarmed.

I had just climbed out of my pup tent when I heard someone coming. I asked for the password and told him to throw down his dog tags. The man turned out to be a rather obnoxious MAO (medical administrative officer) who stepped forward and said, "I'll take charge." At this point, my tongue was sufficiently loosened by the alcohol, and I lost my cool. I said, "No, you won't take charge; I'm in charge."

The next morning the MAO said to me, "You know, Coe, thanks to you I've just been made a fool of at the breakfast table. I am the youngest officer in the entire division, and the incident last night just did not set well with my senior officers." I apologized. Very soon afterward, I found myself crawling on my hands and knees to a field where I vomited from the previous night's abuse of hard cider. After emptying my stomach, I looked up, and there was a jackass, whose field I had stumbled into, looking curiously at me. I remember saying to myself, *I don't know what kind of animal you are, but you're awfully homely.* I gave him an uppercut that landed on the soft spot under his chin. He promptly ran off, no longer curious about me.

As I mentioned, this was my one and only experience with intoxication. What I never understood about that night is the sharpness with which I recall the details of the night's events. If I were to return to Normandy today, I could retrace my same steps from that night and recall every detail.

Comrades L to R: Israel Jaffe, John Irving, Fred Hughes, Yourkanis, and Lee Grille

Our Medics

The Dead Germans

On October 23, 1944, our first day in Holland, we relieved the First Canadian Army. U.S. Major General Terry De La Mesa Allen took command from Canadian Lieutenant General Guy Simonds. We fought near the Holland/Belgium border and the Belgian town of Weisweiler along the northeast highway that ran from Weisweiler to Zunder and Breda. We fought alongside Canadian and British troops.

The military bearing of the Canadians and the English, with respect to discipline and order, always impressed me. On the contrary, the American soldier was somewhat defiant. I am not certain to what degree the military was able to remove or repress the civilian in the American soldier. Perhaps we were not the greatest soldiers from a traditional military standpoint, but we were valiant and dedicated fighters in combat.

Shortly after the 104th division relieved the First Canadian Army, we came across a German panzer (tank) that had been knocked out by previous fighting. The U.S. medical personnel were ordered to remove the dead panzer crew and bury them. We unanimously objected to this order. We were medics. We were prepared to treat the wounded and the sick regardless of their uniform, but we were not the burial detail. This appeared to be a standoff that could have easily resulted in a court marshal for insubordination. I still do not know what would have come of the day if a group of Dutch civilians had not arrived and spontaneously started digging graves.

This German was shot in the head.

First Combat

My first combat exposure was in Holland alongside my fellow medic Nils Isachsen. On October 24, 1944, we were following our platoon to the front when we heard artillery shells. As mentioned earlier, learning to distinguish between incoming and outgoing mail was an initial challenge. It was also during this period that we were first exposed to the V2 rockets. We soon learned that when the motor cut off, an explosion would follow. When the strange-sounding motor cut off, we hit the wet ground and listened to falling shells. About that time, Nils decided that he wanted to empty his bladder. The next shells sounded closer, and I yelled to Nils to hurry up because he didn't want to be found dead holding that thing.

The next shell fell very close, and we found ourselves lying flat on our bellies for the rest of the day on the flat, wet soil of Holland. In relative terms, I don't think we saw any real action that day, but the experience was very real to us. The following day, however, I made my first call to treat and carry a wounded soldier. I can recall carrying him on my shoulders back through the canal. He was so tall that when I carried him, his arms swung freely, dangling past my knees. The water in the canal was so deep that I was able to keep my nose just barely above water. After getting across the canal, two of us then carried the soldier on a litter for what seemed like more than a mile back to the aid station. I was soaking wet and found the staff and officers staying warm around a nice wood fire. With obvious sarcasm, I asked them if it was possible to place the aid station any farther back. The station was so far back that the shelling could only be heard in the far distance. At that point, the MAO took me by the hand and showed me where a shell had hit the aid station. I asked if anyone had been wounded, and he said, "No." I replied, "The reason that you got hit is because you are so damn far back. If you move halfway up to the front, then all these shells will go over your head."

I joined the boys at the fire and gave them my thoughts on combat. I simply stated that there were only three things that could happen: "Number one, you would probably be wounded, or number two, killed, or number three, by some miracle not touched at all." At that point, the captain looked at me and said, "You shut up!" I told him that I came from a free country and thought I should be able to talk freely. After a further exchange of words, he told me that he didn't want me in the outfit. I answered that I was glad because I wouldn't have to look at his ugly face any longer. I was immediately transferred to another outfit. Throughout the war, I continued to hear horrible stories of this company. They always seemed to be in the wrong place at the wrong time and had an extremely high number of fatalities and injuries. I often wonder if this heated interaction and consequential transfer didn't in some odd way save my life.

Much later during the war, when we returned to La Havre, France, to disembark at the Lucky Strike Tent Camp, I saw my original company standing in formation. There was only one soldier that I recognized. For one of the few times in my life my temper (and an ugly captain) had probably saved me from injury or even death. I learned that the medic who replaced me had taken a direct artillery shell and was killed instantly. This reality has caused me to contemplate life and the loss of life many times throughout the years.

Since the war, I have had conversations with some of my medic friends. It is strange how these conversations often turned to the previously mentioned captain and what an obnoxious person he was. I remember more than once thinking that if I were able to go to medical school after the war, I would never use someone like that captain for a role model. In fact, I promised myself not to be like him. I would rather have shared my foxhole with a German than with him. It is strange to realize that while the passage of time usually mellows a person's thoughts and beliefs, in this case, my disdain and dislike for that captain has only increased. On the other hand, there were many admirable captains. We all liked them and would proudly consider many of them role models.

On October 23, 1944, we were finally informed that we were going to relieve the first Canadian army in Holland. Our duty was to help free up the port of Amsterdam. The Allies were in Antwerp, but the Germans had blocked the approaches to it. I recall Lieutenant General G.G. Simonds of the Canadian Forces turning over command to the 104th. I couldn't help but notice the contrast between the Canadian soldiers with their stiff and militaristic bearing and us Americans, who lounged around in a very casual manner. This reaffirmed my thoughts on the contrast in militaristic order between the Canadian and the American armies. I often wondered how much of this was related to culture and how much was training.

I recall one night in Holland that we spent entirely under shellfire. This shellfire was from the 88s (high-speed 88 mm artillery shells). These were high-powered artillery shells with a unique sound that we quickly learned to recognize. Once you hear one, you never forget it. These heavier shells had a very strange wobbling sound as they passed overhead, which made you think that you could almost see them, but, of course, you could not even glimpse them.

Our battalion was in a very bad place from the standpoint of safety. We were in a coffin-shaped foxhole, which was so shallow that the tops of our bodies lay at ground level. There was so much shrapnel flying overhead that we were afraid to get into an upright position in order to dig the foxholes deeper. To make matters worse, trees that lined the road facilitated the scattering of the shell fragments. I recall thinking that anybody in his right mind wouldn't stay here, but leaving would qualify as desertion, so we had no choice but to endure and hope for the best. It was simply luck that none of us were killed that night.

Holland: Our Initial Battle (L to R: A litter-man, Sammy DiCello, and Medic Ron Coe)
Courtesy of Press Photographer, 104th Infantry Division,
Timberwolf Tracks

Outfitting a Medic

The American helmets with plastic liners strapped inside of a metal helmet were, in my opinion, a poor design, but they did provide a level of psychological comfort at the very least. The only way to keep the helmet on was to fasten the chinstrap. When fastened under combat conditions, the force on the inside of the helmet from the concussion of air from exploding shells could create enough force to snap the wearer's neck. We were warned about this, and I never buckled mine during combat.

We once tested the integrity of both a German and an American helmet with a Lugar shot at the helmets. The bullet deflected off the German helmet but went through both sides of the American helmet. It was on these poorly designed helmets that each medic painted the red cross. Initially, we had only Red Cross armbands until we decided to paint the red cross on our helmets. While staying in a Dutch home, we used a drinking glass to trace the circular outline and then painted the red cross. It was typical for the medic to wear one or two armbands and the helmet. Contrary to the Pacific Theater, during wartime in the European Theater, both sides respected the red cross worn by the medic. To the best of my knowledge, none of the European Theater medics were armed, but in the Pacific Theater I understand that they were.

When we started combat in Holland, we had only World War I leggings for our feet. We received combat boots several months after we began active combat. When the cold and rainy weather started, we were issued shoepacks. They looked like someone had cut off a rubber boot just below the knee. They did not breathe and retained moisture very well, which resulted in many cases of trench foot (also called Emerson Foot). Other standard issue clothing were pants, shirts, an army field jacket, helmet, and a raincoat rolled up in our pack and available.

Medics were issued two aid pouches hung from a harness at the neck and shoulders. The pouches could be used fully extended or laced through eyelets to decrease the capacity to half size. Most were used at full capacity. The contents consisted of multiple bandages, prefilled morphine syringes that resemble small tubes of toothpaste with a sterile needle, sulfa powder, bandage scissors, various sizes of clamps, tourniquets, and some nonissued material and medical equipment picked up along the way from German medics. In my opinion, the morphine sulfate used to control an injured soldier's pain was the most important item issued.

City Fighting: Medic Ron Coe
Courtesy of Press Photographer, 104th Infantry Division,
Timberwolf Tracks

Medic Ron Coe

SIW

In Etten, Holland, we were sitting on a living room floor of a private home with our backs against the wall waiting for a jump off. Waiting is often the worst part of an attack. At the opposite end of the room, a rifleman asked for a medic. I went over to him, and he immediately began asking question about combat injuries. He expressed an excessive interest and curiosity about pain control for combat injuries. I explained to him the use and effectiveness of morphine. He seemed satisfied, so I returned to my sitting area. I had only been back in my place a short time when the room was suddenly filled with the sound of an explosion. Most of us thought that a hand grenade had been thrown in from the outside. The explosion was followed by a cry, "Medic, bring the morphine." Sure enough, I found the same rifleman who had recently queried me about pain control crying in pain. I dressed the bullet wound in his foot, and I wrote on the tag, "SIW (self-inflicted wound)—no morphine given." I then gave him a short lecture stating that he would not receive morphine, because in my opinion, it was not to be used for this type of self-inflicted wound. I also informed him that he might face additional charges. He understood and suffered quietly. His relief came from the fact that he was not going into battle.

Common Emotions

It was in Holland that I first encountered a dead German soldier. He lay in a cow barn. Alongside of him were the contents of his wallet, which consisted mostly of photographs that were taken at his wedding and the reception that followed. It hit me that he had apparently been married during a recent furlough back home. I felt sorry for him and for his family. How alike we were in many ways, young men from two different sides of the world living parallel lives. I, too, had been recently married while on my last furlough. Would my wife find herself in the same position as his wife? Out of respect, I removed the German from the muck-collecting pit and laid him to rest in a more peaceful and dignified manner, placing the photos next to his heart.

The Dutch— Forever Friends

One day during combat in Holland I noticed a Dutch civilian approaching. I said to my fellow medic Nils, "I'll bet if that fellow coming toward us could speak English, he would have some sad tales to tell us." To our surprise, he greeted us in English and started to talk of the war and the atrocities being committed by the Germans. They had killed his entire family and burned his house to the ground. This one human interaction seemed to me to justify our presence and the part we played in the war. If ever I had any doubt as to the validity of our purpose, it left me that very day on that flat field in Holland. From that moment on, I faced each day of the war without question.

I was always fascinated by the Dutch, perhaps because of the early stories we read about them during our own childhoods, such as the one about the child with his finger in the dike. During war, the Dutch were consistently fine and gracious people, as I had always imagined. Even many years after the war, these fine people treated us royally. In 1999, we returned to Holland with the 104th veterans. Two villages in a row gave us banquets and presents plus a thank-you talk for our part in the war. In Holland, buildings damaged by the war have been preserved for the children to see in order to reinforce their heritage. We were taken to a street named for the 104th Division, which had been decorated with a plaque honoring the Timberwolves. I commented to one of our Dutch friends that all this seemed a bit much for only two weeks of combat in

Holland. He replied gratefully, "If you had not come, we might all be speaking German." This one comment struck me as profoundly as the comment made to me more than fifty years earlier by the Dutch man regarding the burning of his home and the killing of his family by the German soldiers.

When we visited the graves of our fallen comrades at Margraton, I learned that the Dutch people help to properly maintain them, regularly mowing the grass and planting flowers for birthdays and holidays. They also commemorate their own war heritage with a war museum and park at Overloon.

The visit to Holland was a very rewarding and highly emotional experience. The Dutch have done their share in remembering both the dead and us, the living. My experience in Holland during the war, and again while visiting in 1999, reinforced my positive feelings for the Dutch that I first sensed as a small child. The Dutch are fine people.

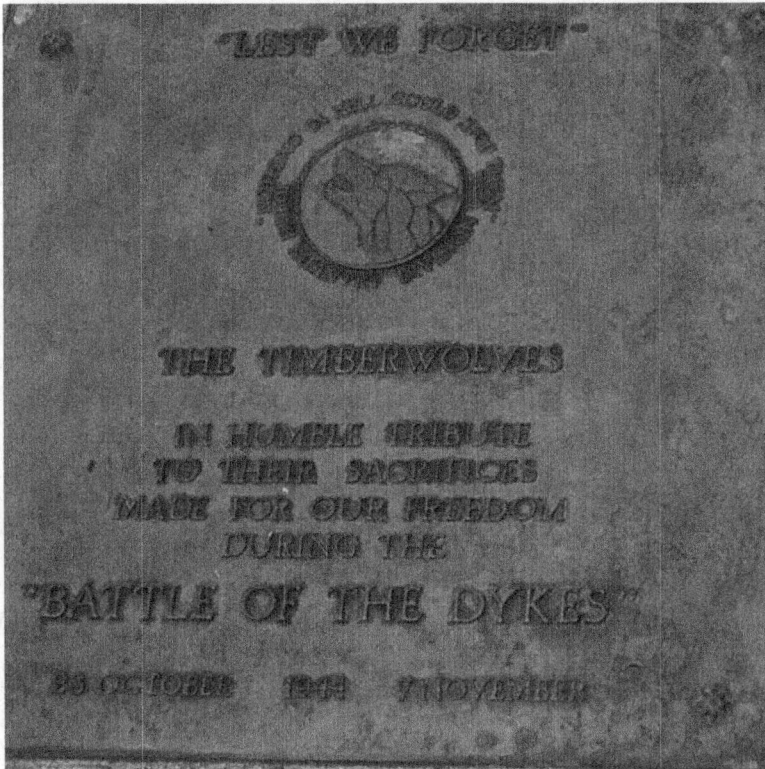

The Apparent Coward

After two weeks of combat in Holland, we took the town of Eschweiler, Germany. We stayed in homes just south of Hill 287 in Stolberg, Germany, while preparing for our attack on the hill and spent five days at the foot of the hill waiting for the weather to clear. While we waited in a private home, we were told that the entire front would move forward at the time of our attack. I recall looking at the kitchen utensils sitting on the kitchen counter and visualizing the owners of the house using them. This was just another way of taking my mind off the impending battle.

From where we stood, I could see a knocked-out American tank among the farmhouses on the hilltop. It had been abandoned there following the previous two failed Allied attacks. Finally the weather cleared, and we watched a massive U.S. Army Air Force attack passing overhead. To our surprise, they did not touch Hill 287; in fact, they went so far beyond it that one could barely hear the rumbling of the distant bombing.

After the U. S. Army Air Force attack passed and just before the first light, we moved toward a forward assembly area. Suddenly, the rifleman in front of me fell to the ground complaining of abdominal pain. The exam was normal with no signs of injury or illness. I sent him back to the aid station, because in his emotional state, he would be of no value to us.

After catching up to my platoon, I made the remark that we were certainly giving the Germans hell. I was told just the opposite was true.

The shelling was all incoming mail (shellfire). After only two weeks of combat in Holland and Belgium, I was still so green that I couldn't tell when shellfire was coming in or going out. When I learned that this was incoming fire, I dug my deepest foxhole ever! Civilians later told us that the enemy routinely shelled the area every morning.

Later, as we started to climb the face of the hill, bullets whizzed past, hitting the barn behind us. As we climbed, I asked my friend Sammy to spread out a bit more because I had confidence that the enemy was not trying to hit a medic; at least I hoped not. Sammy knew my humor well! Early in the war Sammy had self-appointed himself to guard me. He never left my side.

It was at Inden, Germany, while in a factory near the Inde River, that we found ourselves under heavy artillery and rocket fire for an entire night. During the night someone yelled, "Medic, I'm hit." In order to reach the soldier calling out to me, I had to crawl over some burlap bags filled with an unknown substance, which someone told me later was broken crockery. Upon reaching the rifleman, I performed a negative examination and then asked his name. I recognized him as the same soldier that I sent back from the front lines to the aid station the day we had started up Hill 287. Again, I sent him back. This time I hoped that they would never send him to the front again. I doubted if he would ever be able to stand the stress of combat.

I hesitate now to call this soldier a coward. He was not fit for combat and should never have been asked to be there. The passing of years and the accumulation of life experiences make one's judgment more compassionate.

I was always amazed that more soldiers did not break under the intense stress of combat. We all have a breaking point, and it is only a matter of shades of gray. I have been told that some branches of the service (for example, the submariners) do a preselecting test to screen out those prone to high combat stress. The infantry did simulate combat during training in effort to prepare us for combat. Perhaps without us knowing they were doing a form of prescreening. During these sessions, live explosive devices were set off while at the same time machine gunfire traversed overhead. These sessions were more realistic at night and did pose real danger; however, nothing can truly replicate the realities of combat.

Chaplain Clair F. Yohe—Always on Call

I first met Chaplain Yohe during our combat in the Eschweiler-Stolberg area. We were all buttoned up in our foxholes except for the chaplain. At the time, we were under heavy shelling. I watched him as he spiritually administered to the frightened, the wounded, and those who were KIA (killed in action). He appeared to be as calm as if he were giving a routine sermon to a civilian congregation on a Sunday morning. Nonetheless, I climbed out of my foxhole and offered him mine. I told him I could dig another foxhole, and there would be no charge because I was already on salary. He politely refused my offer, replying that he had all the protection he needed. There is an old saying that there are no atheists in foxholes. This display of calmness was beyond my comprehension but was a real inspiration to us.

Later I learned Chaplain Yohe had received a Silver Star, an Oak Leaf Cluster, and a Purple Heart. He not only deserved all of these, but he also deserved an even higher award. His job as a chaplain seemed much more difficult than mine as a medic. While I only treated the wounded and the frightened, he had to meet the needs of every soldier and was always on call. Many years after the war, I tried unsuccessfully to contact him at Isle La Motte, Vermont, where I had heard he was living. If by now he has taken the last bugle call, he should be in a special place for the true believers.

Explosive Power

Initially, upon reaching Hill 287 in Stolberg, Germany, on November 17, 1944, we found several dead horses and cows. This sight always bothered me for two reasons: my love for animals and the constant reminder of the killing power of the various explosive devices. Suddenly, I heard the call, "Medic." In my hurry, I almost ran in front of a line of supine riflemen who were firing into the enemy lines. This was yet another sign of a still green combat soldier. I could have easily lost both of my legs to friendly fire.

There was a large bunker near the top of a hill. When we returned on tour in 1999, this same bunker was being used as a place to keep chickens. Oddly enough, the present occupants were destined to end the same way as the Germans.

Stolberg Bunker, which was the first bunker we saw.

I was searching for a building when an American soldier from another division tapped me on the shoulder. He motioned for me to follow him and guided me to a farmhouse with a warm living room, which was heated by wood. I was surprised to learn that American and German troops were occupying cellars, sometimes just a few yards apart. The latter had recently occupied this space while waiting for us to attack. There was only one thing wrong with the room that had been selected as a waiting place: an extremely large German artillery shell that had come through the wall and not exploded lay resting on an overstuffed rocking chair. It was given a lot of respect and remained there until we left the next day.

We were deep in Germany and walking in very deep mud, which had resulted from a heavy winter snowfall. As we were leaving, I noticed a dapple-gray horse dead on the shed roof, apparently blown up there by a heavy artillery shell. While trying to comprehend what I had just seen and at the same time concentrate on the difficult conditions underfoot, there was a sudden explosion to the right rear. A Jeep had run over a mine, and in the air above it I saw a booted leg, which had been blown off at midthigh level. It was spinning in the air and spiraling up toward the sky like one of those firecracker wheels, but in slow motion. The sight of the dead horse followed by the explosion and a human life blown apart were violent and surreal experiences that left graphic impressions on our young minds.

Many years later, I was talking to my old medic friend Lee Grille. I had remarked that I often wonder if I really saw that spinning leg and also the dead horse on the shed roof. I think I had hoped that these memories where somehow imagined and not real. Grille replied that he vividly recalled both sights. He also remembers seeing me ahead of the Jeep that exploded as he approached it from behind. There is no question at all that we had witnessed this, despite years of trying not to remember.

Some deaths were violent and some peaceful. Despite the way a soldier dies, there is an eerie stillness about a battlefield filled with the dead. I recall checking a large soldier during a battle. He did not have a mark on him, but his legs felt like large, elongated, and intact rubber tubes filled with sand. This was due to the multiple bone fractures from the concussion of a large shell. The soldier was dead, yet he looked so peaceful.

A MEDIC TO A DEAD BUCK PRIVATE

BY GOD, I OUGHT TO BE USED TO THIS
BUT DAMN IT ALL, I NEVER SEE
A DOUGHFOOT DEAD OR DYING IN A HOLE
WITHOUT SOME STAB INSIDE OF ME.

YOU THERE WITH MUDDY ARMS OUTSTRETCHED
WITH BLANK EYES STARING AT THE SKY,
HALF PEACE, HALF TORTURE IN YOUR SPRAWL
THAT SAYS,
OKAY, OKAY I'M DEAD.
BUT WHY?

AND ON THAT BLOODY, GASPING MOUTH
SOME SWEETHEART GAVE HER ARDENT KISSES
TO MATCH YOUR PASSION AND YOUR DEAR
YOUNG DREAMS
ENDED, TOO SOON, LIKE THIS

POOR GUY. YOU CAN'T GO HOME AGAIN
FOR YOU THERE IS NO AFTER,
NO JOB, NO CLEAN WHITE BED NOR SWEET
YOUNG ARMS,
NO SECRET LOVELY LAUGHTER

WELL YOU'RE ANOTHER HERO LAD
A GOLD STARRED WORD FOR DADS AND MOTHERS
BUT YOU WHERE MUCH TO YOUNG TO DIE.
YOU THERE --- AND A MILLION OTHERS

Following World War II, during my last year at Tufts Medical School, I was sitting in one of the professor's offices when I noticed this poem lying under the glass on his desk. I was so impressed and emotionally moved that I copied it onto a stained piece of paper while I sat waiting. I have since been able to research and identify the author as PFC Wesley E. Melton.

Too Much Alcohol

We were in a German house when one of our better riflemen, who'd had too much to drink, started acting strangely and violently. Except for brief and humorous periods when this soldier spontaneously stood at attention and sang the national anthem, there was concern that he would hurt himself or one of us. We needed to somehow quickly subdue him. The only injectable medicine I carried was morphine. I worried about a potential negative effect from the morphine on the respiratory system of someone so intoxicated, so I gave him a small dose—just enough to control his current state. While the violent and strange outbursts were then subdued, the singing was loud and clear, offering continued humor and reassurance for me that the dose of morphine had not been too much.

Following this incident, we captured a small hotel. In the basement of the hotel there was a locked walk-in liquor cage. A quick shot from a comrade's M1 rifle (the standard rifle carried by most soldiers) took care of the lock. Also in the basement near the cage were three elderly German civilians—two females and one very elderly male. We gave them permission to drink the alcohol. Having been deprived of alcohol for most of the war, they began to drink it like coffee or soda. The old man suddenly passed out, causing me initial worry, but thankfully, he survived. Following our many hours in the basement, just as we were leaving, the old man began to sober up. At the very least, I bet those three Germans had good things to say about the Americans and, in particular, our platoon in the hotel basement that day. For my part, I was happy to put behind me a day of administering to the drunk.

The Brave and the Dead

Strange things happen during the intensity and confusion of combat. During a battle in Weisweiler, Germany, I became separated from my platoon and found myself taking care of strangers from another company. One such stranger that I patched up was a Captain Nelson of Company L, a walking wounded man. While a lesser man would have gone back to an aid station on a litter, he was one tough fellow. As he outranked me, he insisted on his right to refuse evacuation to a hospital. Meanwhile, this brave officer could be found cursing madly that he would miss the liquor ration that day due to his injuries. Ultimately, Captain Nelson's injuries necessitated further care, and he did end up in a hospital.

Following my encounter with Captain Nelson, I found myself in the cellar of a German home. The wounded and dead were strewn roughly across the floor—German and American alike. Along the basement wall, I noticed equipment piled on top of American dead. Following my objection, the equipment was quickly removed, and the bodies were straightened. No one should be treated with such disrespect.

As I treated the wounded, one of the Germans caught my attention. When I was close enough to hear clearly, he asked to be sent to a German hospital. I told him otherwise. He was a POW (prisoner of war) and would be sent to an American hospital. I found no need for discussion, as these were our orders for captured troops.

An Old College Foe

At the start of a battle during city fighting, we would often try to select a centrally located building to use as a forward aid station. It was just after dusk when I spotted a suitable building for such a purpose. I started to open the door when along came a tall soldier who pulled down his pants and squatted. I quickly asked him if he could find another location. He stood up, faced me and said, "Coe, do you want to make something of this?" I recognized him as an old ASTP friend from the University of Maine named Herbert Gent. He had been one of the university's athletes who had played against my college (Colby College) before the war. Herb was an imposing figure, even with his pants down around his ankles and everything hanging out. I wisely replied, "No, Herb, finish what you started; we will find another building."

The Capture

After leaving Herb, my buddy Fred Hughes and I opened the basement door of another building that we selected to use as our new forward aid station. We lit a candle to light our way, but we had trouble keeping it lit; when we reached the inside door, the draft blew out the candle. When we finally made our way inside, we found a row of German soldiers ranging from about eighteen to forty years old standing huddled together in the room. They asked us not to shoot them. Of course, they didn't know we couldn't shoot anyone or anything with only medical equipment. In their helmets, the German soldiers had neatly stored their beet sugar and all of their personal effects. We walked outside with them and handed them over to the armed troops. One old German soldier pleaded with us not to take the watch that his mother had given to him. I asked the boys to leave it alone, which they did. I suspect someone along the way did remove the watch; however, I always hoped they hadn't done so. Despite our role as enemies, there were daily reminders, such as the one given by this soldier, that we were all men with mothers, fathers, wives, brothers, and sisters. We were simply born on opposing teams.

We heard later that these Germans could not fire their rifles because they were filled with cosmoline, a thick, protective substance to prevent rust. It was ironic that neither these German soldiers nor Fred and I, as medics, were armed with fatal weapons. Fred and I were lucky but also careless entering that cellar alone and unarmed—not too smart.

Medics Ron Coe and Fred Hughes

The Legging

We had just finished one of our fiercest and most prolonged fights. When it was over, we withdrew to what was left of a fairly large city. I was walking down the street when the MP (military police) on duty informed me that I was out of uniform because I was wearing only one legging. We were still wearing World War I leggings and had not yet received our combat boots. The MP took me to a colonel who was sitting in his plush office. The colonel reiterated that I was out of uniform and asked if I had an explanation for such improper conduct. I told him that the legging had been used to immobilize a soldier's fractured arm, an injury he'd received in active combat. I felt that my legging was probably doing more good where it was than if it had remained on my leg. I went on to describe to the colonel the details of active combat. I doubted if he had any idea what combat was like. He abruptly dismissed me with the order to obtain another legging. I answered, "Yes, sir," saluted him, and left. I often wondered if he collected a battle ribbon while sitting in that office.

Medic Ron Coe outfitted in World War I leggings.

The Sergeant

I recall the sergeant as an unpleasant fellow. He was one of the original Timberwolves. He didn't seem to like anyone, and he wasn't liked by anyone. Not only was this sergeant a poor leader in combat who lacked respect for and from the soldiers under his command, but he also set poor examples for his soldiers. Following battles, he would raid the packs of soldiers killed in action.

I recall a skirmish we were in when our lieutenant told the sergeant under his command to lead the way. The sergeant pulled a rifle, pointed it at the lieutenant, and said, "No, you lead the way." At gunpoint, the lieutenant followed his subordinate's order.

During one of our attacks, we were receiving help from rear overhead machine-gun fire when a stray bullet killed the sergeant. No one shed a tear, but at least no one raided his personal belongings. I wondered at the time, and often still wonder, if it was friendly fire that killed him.

The Moving Dead

The number of dead Germans increased as we continued fighting. It is strange how certain dead soldiers remain forever fixed in your mind. One such German soldier had been shot at a railroad crossing. We spent two or three days in that same area, and it seemed that every time I looked at him he was in a different position. It was as though he lived and moved in death. The movement, of course, was due to the looters who left him in yet another posture of death each time they passed by.

Vigilante Justice

We once freed some Polish workers in a factory. After they were freed, the workers promptly beat the factory's overseer to death. We did not interfere. Perhaps this seems inhuman, but at the time, most of us showed no emotion. They knew what they were doing and instinctively, we did not judge them. By that time, we had experienced so much and lost so many close friends that we were in a constant state of numbness. This is not an excuse, but it is the way things were at that time in our lives.

No matter how tough a situation is there is always room for humor—a great aid to survival. Following the incident above, we noticed two horses in a pasture that were trying to mate. The penis on the horse looked about the size of a large man's arm. It seemed to be plowing the dirt and not going anywhere. One of our soldiers, apparently an old farm boy, walked over and guided it into its proper place. He was loudly applauded. Despite the killing, nature has a way of keeping a balance. The animals, like the humans, were now replenishing their species after all the killing.

Photo found in a German home

Political Power

At the starting point of our drive to Cologne, Germany, on November 6, 1944, we were loaded into Dodge trucks for our transfer to Aachen, Germany. A sergeant was standing at the tailgate calling out our names as we boarded. One soldier with a well-known political name from an East Coast family was just about to climb aboard when the sergeant said, "Hold it. You are going to spend the remainder of the war in a rest camp running the movie projector." The "political powers" can have long protective arms, giving this young man a position in the war with virtually guaranteed safety. The rest of us continued to board the transport trucks destined for the front lines.

The BAR Rifleman

Somewhere near Aachen, Germany, riding in the back of a truck, I had a long, friendly talk with a soldier from Pennsylvania. He told me of his last trip home before being sent back overseas. He'd spent a good deal of time hunting with his father, an Army colonel who was on leave at the same time. As we talked, he sat with his BAR (Browning automatic rifle) cradled in his arms.

That night we were pinned down by artillery fire in a relatively small wooded area. We sustained many casualties, and the next morning I was saddened by the sight of a number of frozen dead bodies being thrown into an Army truck like cordwood. Among the dead, I saw the automatic rifleman with his arms folded, flexed as if he were still holding his weapon. Initially, I thought of his mother who had to face this tragic loss of her son. Through the years my thoughts have focused not only on the soldier's mother but also on his father, the colonel.

War leaves one with fragmented thoughts and vivid images that persist throughout life. I still remember in great detail this BAR rifleman, stacked among the other frozen casualties while his fellow East Coaster sat safely running the movie projector far from enemy fire. The BAR rifleman was not lucky enough to have political power or the protection that it brought to a lucky few.

The Wrong Gold Star Mother

A gold star mother is one whose child was killed in action. It was during combat in Inden, Germany, that our sergeant was taking the daily census of the dead for his report. We were in a large factory where there were several soldiers KIA, and the sergeant had identified all of the dead except for one. He asked for the name of this last soldier, and someone gave him a name, which he later learned to be an incorrect one. The error was due to the fact that the sergeant did not double-check the dead soldier's dog tag. I never knew for sure but always wondered if a mother had been misinformed of her son's death. I hope not.

The Apparent Brave

During a lull in combat while in Germany, I had just finished developing some photographs when one of the platoon members walked into my makeshift darkroom. He showed me a picture of his family and then asked me what was wrong with the picture. It appeared to be a nice family picture. He asked me to concentrate my focus on the youngest child in the picture. Between sobs he told me that his best friend had fathered the youngest child. The following day when we were fighting the Germans, the same fellow went way out on a point into active combat for no apparent reason. At the time it appeared to be either a very brave or foolish action.

That night I learned the truth. He had become so upset over his wife's infidelity that he was hoping that the Germans would kill him. This must have been a rare case of apparent bravery that was not brave at all.

I had a long talk with this soldier about a recent relationship he had. We were in active combat at the time when he met a pretty German lady. She was playing classical music at a piano on the top floor of a roofless apartment house. The roof had been blown off during combat. I told him that in my opinion what his wife did was not much different than what he had done. I never saw him do anything abnormal again, and I think he made it through the war alive. Despite this soldier's apparent bravery that day on the point, I hope that he was able to maintain a fair perspective each time he thought about his wife's actions and reflected upon his own.

Half-Truths Plus an Amazing Response

Inden, Germany, stands out in my mind as the site of one of the heaviest and most intense shelling incidents we encountered. There was a combination of artillery and rocket fire all around us. We found ourselves in a small industrial complex, which was filled with many wounded soldiers. I recall hearing one soldier cry out in broken English, "I got a piece; I got a piece." He had a lower abdominal puncture wound that made me suspect he was bleeding into the urinary bladder. He calmed down after the administration of morphine. His wound appeared to be serious, but I implied otherwise in order to calm him down and get him evacuated to the aid station in the rear. As with most combat injuries, the medic seldom knows the outcome for those treated in the field and is often left wondering, sometimes even later in life.

Another soldier had sustained shrapnel wounds, and his foot was attached mostly by skin. He asked me if he would lose his foot. I gave him a vague answer. For some reason after the war, I found his name in a book I had been keeping. I was in an area of upstate New York near where he lived when I stopped at a phone booth and started to dial his number. However, I could not complete the call. I thought that he would not understand why I was less than honest regarding the prognosis of his foot or perhaps I could not face seeing this man without his foot. I still feel badly about my vague answer that day in the field.

Since the war and during my own practice of medicine, I have been guilty of some half-truths. I guess this falls under the art of practicing medicine with sensitivity to the human soul.

It was in this same factory complex in Inden that a soldier was bleeding profusely. He was becoming weaker and finally lapsed into shock and was completely unresponsive. I asked another soldier to go back to the aid station for a couple of units of plasma and was relieved when he returned with them.

I quickly started one unit of plasma, which immediately revived the wounded man. Following the second unit, the previously unresponsive soldier was awake and joking with us and also eating. It was there on that battlefield, as I knelt beside this soldier, that my thoughts returned to my previous plans of studying medicine. This experience had a maturing effect on me, and I vowed that day to study harder if I survived combat. I would return to Colby College, finish my premed studies, and make, without question, a lifelong commitment to help those in need of medical care.

The Minefield

We were deep in Germany while under artillery and mortar fire when a call went out, "Medic, wounded up ahead." I advanced toward the call for help. As I recall, the ground underfoot was slightly frozen but still spongy. I found two wounded soldiers who appeared to have stepped on mines. I noticed some tank tracks and tried to walk cautiously in them as much as possible to avoid potential mines. I carried the smaller soldier first and then went back for the tall soldier. The second soldier was so tall that his hands and feet dragged on the ground. This was a challenging carry made even more so as I tried to stay in the tank tracks. My main fear was that the added weight of the soldier on my back would set off another mine. The partially frozen ground may have prevented this from happening. As I approached the line of riflemen firing at the enemy, one of them looked up and said, "Hey, Doc, who do you think you are, Atlas?" It was for my effort on this day that I was awarded the Silver Star.

Somehow, I later learned that Lieutenant William Perry had written the citation for my Silver Star. This knowledge gave my Silver Star added value because it would always remind me of this brave and outstanding lieutenant.

Words Better Left Unspoken

On the evening of January 15, 1945, we were on the autobahn moving up to the front line near the Roer River in Germany. During a short rest, the soldier in front of me slammed a mortar case filled with shells onto the cement highway. I was not concerned over the ammunition, but rather the noise. I told the mortar shell carrier that if he did this again the Germans would not have to kill him because one of us would.

Late that night we finally moved into a house on the Roer River opposite Duren. This house was quiet and built like a fortress. The basement was similar to a pillbox with heavy cement overhead. The sentries were posted, and we settled down for the night. Suddenly, the silence was broken by the sound of rifle fire followed by the cry, "Medic." At the top of the stairs, I found our mortar shell carrier lying on the floor. In the darkness I started to examine him, and I soon realized that my fingers were inside his skull and covered with his blood and brain tissue. As I turned at the top of the stairs, I noticed a full-length mirror leaning against the wall. Our mortar shell carrier had been standing in front of it and in the moonlight probably looked like at least two people. At the foot of the stairs, I found our sergeant, who had fired the fatal shot when there was no response to his requests for the password. I did my best to console this brave and outstanding noncom (noncommissioned officer).

The following night this same sergeant was returning to our side of the river, leading his squad, which was being chased by Germans. He correctly called for protective artillery fire, but the shells fell short and killed him just as he was entering our backyard. That same day he had been promoted to staff sergeant.

During the overseas trip with the 104th Division Veterans in May 1999, I found myself compelled to search the military cemeteries for the graves of these two men. I located the sergeant's grave and quietly reflected, mourned, and praised this fine soldier. Regretfully, I could not locate the mortar shell carrier's grave.

I often remember those two brave soldiers who were each victims of friendly fire. I recall the words I said to the mortar shell carrier that night on the autobahn—words that would have been better left unspoken. Many war experiences fade or vanish with the passing of time, but this one remains as clear today as if it occurred yesterday.

Hand-to-Hand Combat— No Thanks

During our time on the Roer River opposite Duren, Germany, we were alerted to a possible German breakthrough just to the right of where we were. Many of us doubted that this could possibly be true. Despite our doubt, we were on high alert one evening. One of our outposts was a small building with a screened-in porch where there were several bicycles. That night the soldier on duty heard a noise on the porch. It turned out to be a German soldier tripping over one of the bikes. The American and the German looked at each other, and suddenly, each turned and ran in opposite directions. Neither one wanted to risk the feel of cold steel or even a bullet. I hope that they both lived to tell the story.

The breakthrough we had scoffed at did happen. It was called the Battle of the Bulge.

A "Boarding House" in Brussels

During periods when combat was at a lull, the army would grant passes, which temporarily relieved us of our duties. One such lull occurred while our division was stationed along the Roer River in Germany. Several of us obtained three-day passes and traveled to Brussels. We paid for a seemingly adequate room at a boarding house and were happily surprised by the cheap rate. Our satisfaction with the room did not last long, however, as we were awakened many times throughout the night by the sound of slamming doors. In the morning we inquired about the previous night's interruptions. The house manager replied that they were also running "another type of business." We left laughing as we realized we had spent the night in a whorehouse. We finally knew why the rate was so cheap.

The famous Market Square in Brussels

"Manikin Piss"—famous statue in Brussels

The Beer Keg

During the period we spent on the Roer River and during a lull in fighting, we were able to find a keg of beer in a local brewery. We sat facing the river while enjoying the keg. All of us had taken turns to fill pitchers of beer without incident, and then one fellow went out to fill a pitcher and was killed by a mortar shell. As I examined him, strange thoughts raced through my mind. I thought about how he would never again enjoy the taste of beer, let alone the beer in the pitcher he had just filled. Many years later even the smallest sip of beer brings back the memory of this day on the Roer River and the ill-fated death of our comrade. One evening during the same period of time, another fellow went outside to empty his bladder. He just stepped out of the door and was killed. I can't believe the Germans had any forward observation station because there were buildings between the river and us. I have come to believe that these deaths were just unlucky timing for our soldiers and a stroke of good luck for the Germans.

The Beer Pitcher

Unexpected Room Service

During our long stay on the edge of the Roer River, Sammy and I slept in the basement of a house. One morning Lieutenant Powell woke us with a knock on our door and served us breakfast in bed. Lieutenant Powell had replaced Lieutenant Perry. Oddly, both lieutenants were alike in that they both cared for the welfare of the enlisted men and were themselves very brave in combat.

We were lucky to have had two outstanding lieutenants. They were real leaders and gentleman officers. Both lieutenants were killed in action. One evening Lieutenant Powell stepped into a factory courtyard and was killed by enemy shelling. Lieutenant Perry was killed in Inden, Germany, when he opened a basement door as the Germans fired up the stairwell. Sammy was right behind Lieutenant Perry and returned rifle fire down the stairwell. Sammy was not very tall and can probably thank his short stature for his survival. We had lost two of the finest and bravest line officers, Lieutenant William E. Perry and Lieutenant Ross E. Powell. They're gone but not forgotten.

Sammy

Combat depletes the troops. This is a natural and sad fact of war. Sever (Sammy) DiCello, PFC was in the initial group of replacements we received. A barber in civilian life, he was born in southern Italy and had become an American citizen just in time to be drafted. We were friends from our initial meeting. He was always at my side in all the combat we experienced. I basically trusted the Germans from the standpoint of them respecting the red cross that I wore; nevertheless, it was comforting to have someone with a rifle or a carbine by my side. Sammy favored the carbine. He was remarkably cool under fire and never showed fear, no matter how heavy the shelling. In fact, during our last half of combat, Sam exchanged his helmet for one of those soft tanker hats that fastened under the chin. I suggested that he put his helmet back on, but he replied, "The Germans don't have any firepower left." Just then, a shell hit very close, and I said, "What do you think that was?" His response, "Well, they don't have very much left."

It was at Inden, Germany, that Sammy accompanied me across the Inde River where I would patch up two machine gunners on the other side. As we were crossing back over the bridge upon our return, a shell hit nearby, and we both hit the deck. For his bravery in accompanying me on this mission, I wrote Sammy up for a Silver Star (for bravery in action), and it was awarded. In my opinion, it was beyond the call of duty for a rifleman to accompany a medic on missions like the one just described.

Sam: There was none braver.

Sammy was wounded twice. The first time he set off one of our own hand grenades that had a trip line attached between a house and a dead horse's leg. I called him a klutz. The second wound occurred while we were riding the Third Armored tanks. The Germans had set one of our ammunition trucks on fire. We were lying face down behind the tank turret, and just as our tank reached the truck, a shell exploded, and shrapnel hit Sammy in the rear. I tossed a little alcohol on the wound just to get a rise out of him.

When I think about Sammy, I recall a time while we were still riding the tanks. We stopped at a railroad station, and the phone rang. Sam picked up the receiver and heard two German ladies talking about the American panzers. Sammy just said into the mouthpiece, "*Dummkopf!*"

My friendship with Sammy is one of those friendships that lasts a lifetime. Years ago, our two families went to the New York World's Fair together. We traveled between Ohio and Connecticut several times to visit each other and continued to see each other throughout the years.

Early one Sunday morning, many years after the war, someone was throwing stones at the bedroom window of our house. Although not an everyday occurrence, I told my wife I was not getting out of bed for anyone. She said, "There are two men out there, and one is holding a rock the size of a golf ball." That changed my mind. One was Sammy, and the other was his friend. The previous day, Sam, a barber in civilian life, was cutting his friend's hair when the friend offered to drive through the night from Ohio to Connecticut so that Sammy could visit with us. Our bond was transparent.

Some years later, Sam came to Vermont to visit us. He said that if he had his barber tools he would give me a haircut just like during the war. I immediately pulled out a box of barber equipment and got my haircut. He said, "This is good equipment; what do you have it for?" I said, "Oh, I use it to trim my schnauzer."

This was the last time I saw Sam. In 2004, I received a long distance and long-dreaded phone call from his family to tell me that Sammy, who had been ill for a long time, had passed on. Memories of Sammy will always be with me.

Sammy DiCello and Ron Coe—many years later!

T4 Jess T. Renteria

Jess was from Pueblo, Colorado, and was one of the three aid men in our company. An aid man accompanies the troops wherever they go in combat; they administer first aid and medical care. Controlling bleeding and pain and offering emotional support are primary responsibilities. The aid man often uses morphine to control pain and administers plasma to those in shock. They assist the litter bearers in transporting the wounded to a safer area. An aid man can pronounce and tag a soldier KIA. If the soldier is transported to advanced care, the aid man may never know the final results of their efforts. Aid men also treated the wounded enemy when necessary.

In my opinion Jess was the best and the greatest aid man. Following one of our most intense battles, Jess received the Distinguished Service Cross for exceptional service in a position of great responsibility and danger. This was well deserved. The very fact that he was in our company gave me confidence that if I were seriously wounded, he would be there to care for me. Jess was my role model and my good friend.

Medics L to R: Fred Hughes, Israel Jaffe, Ron Coe, and Jess Renteria

Jim

Sergeant Jim Boyle was one fine soldier and a friend. He and a fellow Timberwolf were captured by the Germans while delivering a message on the front lines in Weisweiler, Germany. Jim had escaped injury, but his friend did not. Jim was helping his injured friend hop back to safety when they were both captured. A young German soldier immediately ordered Jim to put his buddy down. Then the German pulled a door off the hinges from a local house and said to Jim in broken English, "Now we carry him together." The Germans, too, could show compassion.

Jim remained a prisoner for most of the remainder of the war. I did not see Jim again until the very end of the war when another American division freed him from captivity. The officer in charge of the division that freed him offered to find the Timberwolves, but Jim refused the help and walked alone out of the prison camp. He walked a few blocks down the road and found us out of sheer luck. "The luck of the Irish," I told him. I never once asked him about his time in the prison camp.

I saw him not long after the war during a visit to Boston, Massachusetts. He had been discharged early and brought home some German medical equipment for me. We continued to see each other during his visits to Connecticut and also to Vermont. I said my final goodbye to him at the time of his passing.

Fred

My friend and fellow medic Fred Hughes was a paradox. He could irritate you without much effort, but we all liked him. Once he risked heavy shellfire by crossing an open field to the aid station to bring back a care package sent to me from home. He was very brave, especially when he was hungry! We all enjoyed the package, thanks to Freddie and my Aunt Marion who had sent it.

Fred had seen pictures of my wife, Eleanor. Whenever we were getting ready for a combat jump off, he would come up behind me and in a low monotone would say, "Coe, this time they will kill you, and I will go home and marry Eleanor." Then it was Freddie's turn to go after some wounded. Of course, it was also my turn to tell him that he certainly would be killed. Thankfully, he was not. This all seems so heartless and cold now, but it was one of the ways we dealt with reality.

At Inden, Germany, we came across several wounded Germans in a factory. Whenever we captured an area with wounded German soldiers, we checked them daily and gave them the same treatment as our own. At Inden, Freddie and I were checking the wounded Germans when he noticed a German soldier with his eyes open and his hands clasped behind his head, apparently staring at us. Freddie pointed out that the German did not respond to painful stimulus such as pinching of the toes. I told Fred that dead people do not feel pain. Fred had a very light complexion, but suddenly, he looked even paler than the dead German.

Medic Fred Hughes

A couple of gentlemen with canes—Ron Coe and Fred Hughes

The Fully
Intoxicated Soldier

During our drive to Cologne, K Company of the 414th Regiment was facing the enemy across a flat, open plain with dense forest covering an elevated ridge in the distance. A familiar call could be heard, "Medic, wounded up ahead." I started across the flat land, and as I moved near the ridge, I noticed a cement bridge wide enough for a two-lane road. Suddenly, a GI approached walking slowly toward me. He did not appear to be in any distress, but I ultimately realized that he was intoxicated. I asked if he knew of any wounded in the area calling for help. He pointed to his neck and replied, "Perhaps you are looking for me?" I asked him what happened, and he told me that he had been looking for a German tank to attack with his carbine grenade launcher when he was shot in the neck. The examination revealed a small entrance wound on the anterior with a slightly larger exit wound on the posterior. The wounds were clean and not bleeding. The bullet had missed the trachea, the major vessels, the cervical spinal cord, the vertebrae, and the nerves. Returning to our line, my new patient noticed two young German prisoners who were really only children. He suddenly pulled out his trench knife and started to cut off their coat buttons. Upon reaching the top of the coat, he tickled their necks with the knifepoint and stole a German helmet. I jumped between him and these children and took the knife. The GI climbed into the back seat of the waiting and open Jeep wearing the German prisoner's helmet.

I can still see the vision of this American GI wearing the German helmet as he rode away. I often wonder if he made it back without being mistaken for an enemy soldier and getting killed by friendly fire. The odd thing is that not one of us thought to remove the helmet. In my experience intoxicated soldiers were rare in combat. They not only endanger themselves but also everyone else around them.

Diarrhea

We were on the Cologne Plain in Germany chasing the Germans when we spotted an open spring. With intense and abundant thirst, we scrambled toward the spring. After I finished satisfying my thirst, the next soldier got down on his belly and said, "Coe, did you see the dead moldy rat at the bottom of this spring?" I thought he was joking, but a closer look verified the rat's presence. At this point, and without hesitation, I forced myself to vomit.

Most likely, the severe and prolonged diarrhea and high temperature that lasted for the following several days was related to the contaminated water. At sick call, I was given a repeat prescription of the same medication to control the diarrhea. I informed the captain that it was ineffective, but if it made him happy I would take it again. At this point, I drank the entire bottle of anti-diarrhea medication, much to the chagrin of the captain. After I made my point clear, he asked me how severe the diarrhea was. I turned away from him and dropped my pants to show him the feminine pad I was wearing. I have a vague recollection of someone checking me that night. I was somewhat delirious with fever and asked them not to cross my arms because I feared that I would be placed in a coffin, as I probably looked nearly dead.

Chancellor Bismarck

On February 23, 1945, after sitting for an extended period of time on the Roer River opposite Duren, Germany, we moved out. It was two or three hours after midnight when we made the move under the cover of heavy artillery fire. We had an uneventful crossing except that several of our boats tipped over because of the flooded river. When we reached Duren, there was hardly a building standing, and the smell of death was everywhere. I still recall seeing a woman's hand stretched out from the edge of the rubble. She had almost made it. In the center of the town square, which was now completely flattened, the only thing standing was a bronze statue of Chancellor Bismarck. The statue had spun about 190 degrees, so the chancellor was nearly facing the opposite direction from his original position. I also recall his sword had been broken off!

As we approached Cologne, I remember seeing the Olympic stadium where the American runner Jesse Owens had won his event so soundly while Hitler watched—an event I had seen pictures of in the newspapers in 1936. The prominent twin spires of the Cologne Cathedral were visible from a distance. White flags signaling surrender hung from many of the windows in town. Some of the German civilians stood holding white flags. Civilian resistance would hardly have been possible, because we rode through town on tanks. While some areas were completely destroyed, I was surprised that some of the beautiful homes along the Rhine were barely touched by the bombings. We made our quarters there in some of those homes. I can remember soldiers throwing out furniture because it was in our way and how bothered I was by their actions. I couldn't help but think about how hard these people must have worked to obtain that furniture and how quickly it was discarded. Valuable objects have little value during a war. The same could be said of human life.

Cologne Cathedral Twin spirals seen in the distance.

The Disturbed Dead

The Cologne Cathedral appeared to have only a little damage, yet there was clear evidence that a battle had ensued in the cathedral's immediate vicinity. Directly outside the front door of the cathedral was a damaged American tank that was no longer functional. Many say that the survival of the cathedral was due to either divine providence, the accuracy of the bombing, or perhaps superior skill of the medieval craftsmanship.

It was in the Cologne area that I recall seeing a cemetery with many of its coffins and some of the dead who had been buried in them exposed and above ground. At the time, this really bothered me, and to this day, it remains a vivid and haunting recollection. I refuse to believe that even the most sadistic person would deliberately bomb a cemetery. War does not leave even the dead alone.

Cologne Cathedral

A Pleasant Breakfast

Toward the end of the battle in Cologne, Germany, when we were moving and changing locations rapidly—fighting in both the country and in the city—clearing the buildings of the Germans was just a formality. Somehow I had moved ahead of our troops without realizing it. I entered an apartment and found an elderly German couple eating breakfast. They invited me to join them, and I accepted their offer, adding some of my K-rations (dehydrated food issued to soldiers). It was my experience that the older Germans were less apt to show animosity toward us. Shortly after joining this couple at their breakfast table, two of our rifleman barged in with their rifles drawn expecting action. I asked them to put down their toys and join us. Without questioning, they did just that and even contributed some of their K-rations to the morning meal. It was a delightful experience in the midst of combat. After sharing our rations with our hosts, we finished breakfast, and I exchanged a pleasant glance with them. Were these folk any different than my own grandparents? In times like this, the war experience is strange and even pleasant.

City Ruins

Country Ruins

The Railroad Shell

On March 10, 1945, an enemy 16-inch railroad shell hit the 414th regimental command post. The high-ranking officers had just come up out of the cellar when a shell landed in the kitchen and struck and killed our regimental commander (Colonel Anthony Tourat), another colonel, and a lieutenant colonel. Eleven others were wounded. The amazing fact is that the shell did not explode. This seems to me to be a simple example of being in the wrong place at the wrong time.

Life with the Third Armored

On March 22, 1945, the 414th regiment joined the Third Armored Division at the Remagen Bridgehead in Cologne, Germany. We were under the command of the tankers and General Maurice Rose, the commander of the Third Armored Division. He and I had one thing in common in that we were both born in Middletown, Connecticut. To the best of my knowledge, he was the only division commander of the Allies who was killed in action—most likely because he spent far more time with his troops on the frontlines. General Rose was being taken prisoner during combat when a young German officer, apparently quite nervous at the time, thought the general was reaching for his sidearm and shot him to death. In reality, the general was following the German's orders to turn over his sidearm.

Original Bridge at Remagen

Temporary Pontoon Bridge at Remagen

Our two divisions would ultimately travel three hundred miles together on these tanks. We were compatible from the beginning and maintained a high level of mutual respect. The very thought of riding on the outside of an M4 Sherman tank was itself frightening. Initially, the only thing I knew about our tanks was that they were faster than the German panzers. However, I also knew that the German panzers had more firepower and heavier armor than the American tanks.

I likened the Timberwolves riding on the outside of these tanks to birds riding a rhinoceros. It was amazing how quickly we adjusted to traveling on the tanks. It seemed like a symbiotic relationship. As time went on, it even became possible for us to sleep on the tanks during travel. The mutual respect between the tankers and the Timberwolves, coupled with our quick adjustment to tanker life, was remarkable.

On March 25 we headed toward Marburg and Paderborn. As we stared off into the night, we could see our tracers (bullets) setting house curtains, houses, and especially barns on fire. It was an unforgettable sight. During this journey, we had to stop frequently to clear trees from the road that had been deliberately placed to block our way. While traveling and heading toward Paderborn, Germany, sixty miles north of Marburg, we engaged in several battles along the way.

After traveling two hundred miles on these tanks, we crossed the Weser River at dusk and approached the small peaceful-appearing town of Wewer. Sam and I were riding the lead tank, which changed every day. It was on March 31, as we approached this small peaceful-appearing village, that suddenly all hell broke loose. We were hit by bazooka fire during intense hand-to-hand combat. I learned later that the three tankers behind us were also hit. This was the most intense fighting in a close area that I experienced. Yet, despite such active fighting, I was amazed to see the hatch doors of our tanks open more often than closed during battle.

It turned out that this little town housed a training camp for young SS troopers. Live action was all around us when suddenly I found myself lying on the ground near the tank that I had been riding. I never figured out if I was knocked clear off the tank or if I jumped off. Out of at least ten soldiers on the tank I was the only one not injured, thanks to my protective colleagues. They had a way of protecting "Doc" by deliberately surrounding me. My safety was a direct result of my comrades' and my friends' relentless protection. At times, they literally protected my body with their own.

The Germans were ready and waiting for us in every alley. As we traveled, we would pass through towns with German military vehicles parked outside the houses. The infantry riding in trucks behind us would sometimes engage in battles with the German military within these houses.

While we traveled, we had air force coverage, which included an Air Corps officer, who had direct contact with the planes overhead, riding in the tanks. There were colored plastic markers on the top rear of the tanks, which identified us to the U.S. Army Air Corps as friendly American tanks. The markers were changed daily for security. I recall being in pursuit of a German panzer when an American plane flew toward us and suddenly pulled up, wiggling his wings. The system to identify our own tanks had worked. One night we were riding through the forest when I awoke suddenly and saw overhead the cranelike structure of a tank recovery vehicle that was about to push us off the mountain road. In sheer fright, I broke the blackout restriction and flashed my light. The tank recovery vehicle stopped just in time.

We finally caught up with the German panzer, which by then had already been successfully knocked out by the American planes. There is no question that throughout the war concentrating on the wounded allowed me to block out such intense fighting as the tankers often engaged in.

We reached Paderborn, Germany, after traveling 193 miles in nine days passing some of the most beautiful German countryside. While the countryside was beautiful, the experience represented the most intense and exciting period of combat for me. I hesitate to describe war in such a way, yet I often found the intensity to be stimulating and, in an odd way, exciting. Being on the edge of death made us feel intensely alive.

A German Burial

While riding the Third Armored tanks on an overcast and rainy day, we passed a small group of elderly civilians climbing a hill carrying a coffin to the cemetery. We did not need such a reminder of death, as we were approaching a battle. If the deceased civilian was elderly, he or she had almost survived two wars. If the deceased was younger, we might have been responsible for his death. The deceased may have contributed to the wartime death count before his own death. Regardless, I was certain that before sundown we would most likely add to or be added to the day's mortality list.

We're Human Beings

We stopped one night by a church that had a sign proudly announcing the fact that "Silent Night" had been composed right there at that church. I can remember thinking what a paradox it was that such a peaceful song had been composed in a spot currently surrounded by anything but silence and peace. One day, while the memory of this church remained fresh in my mind, I was sitting on a tank watching a dogfight overhead through German Army field glasses. I watched an American fighter pilot shoot down a German plane, followed by the German pilot's gentle and quiet float to the ground as he parachuted to safety. The violence of war followed by the pilot's peaceful landing reminded me yet again of the continued paradox of silence, peace, and violence all wrapped together and seen through the German field glasses' lens.

It was through these same field glasses that I saw my first German jet. I remember wondering at the time if the Germans had jets before the Americans. I later learned this to be true. While the action was going on above, I noted out of the corner of the lens a German woman far on the horizon lift her skirt, squat, and urinate. This sight offered an amusing contrast to war and a clear reminder that we were fighting in the midst of daily life and that we were all human beings whose lives in peacetime were clearly very similar.

Further reminders of how alike we all were occurred near the end of the war. I remember walking near the end of a long line of German prisoners. I struck up a conversation with two former German law students whose studies had been interrupted by the war. They were very friendly and cooperative. I was not fearful walking with them. Being a medic, I was, of course, unarmed and being prisoners they, too, were unarmed. They said that they had been placed in the army without choice. I had no reason to doubt this. Most of us Americans had also been drafted or had enlisted in a reserve unit. I often wish I had asked their names and reconnected later in life. This was just one more reminder that we were all simply human beings who were more alike than we were different.

A Quick Response

We had just emerged from a mountain road when the lead tank spotted an 88 artillery gun emplacement. Our tank gunner turned suddenly and shot the opposing crew. Later, when our troops checked the gun sight of the 88, we found it was pointing directly at the lead tank.

While still with the tankers, we were watching the enemy, who was situated a long distance away across the valley in a building. I asked the gunner if he could put a shell in the basement window. This distance would have been a good shot for an M1 rifle. He did this without disturbing the stonework. The surviving enemy soldiers ran to get under a truck when our gunner fired another shell, setting the truck on fire. There were no signs of life after this.

No Time to Heal

One of the original tanker soldiers from the Third Armored had a boil on his face. I was treating the boil with wet hot packs. One morning I went to check him when another tanker stopped and told me that I didn't have to worry about caring for the first tanker's infection any more. During the night, a shell had landed near the tank turret and blown off the wounded soldier's head. My immediate reaction was that this was a sick joke, but in reality, I was never to see that soldier again.

A Confession

I had learned to use a rifle in basic training, even though I was a noncombatant. I recall using three different models. Initially, I barely qualified using the English Enfield, which had no lateral wind correction. With the second rifle, a Springfield, I scored sharpshooter. I then scored in the expert range with the third rifle, which was a U.S. Army MI. Army medics did not carry weapons and were not expected to use them.

For some unexplained reason, on March 29, 1945, our tanks had an unusually long stop on our way to Wewer, Germany. The tank on which I rode parked close to a German ammunition dump. Instinctively, I did not take my eyes off that ammunition dump area. Suddenly, I spotted a German soldier moving toward the ammunition. Without thinking, and I suppose with an innate survival instinct, I grabbed Sammy's carbine, which had been resting on the tank turret. I had the German in my sight and was just about to press the trigger when I came to my senses. I was an Army medic charged with caring for the wounded, not inflicting a wound. Mine would have been a sure shot. I handed the weapon to Sammy and told him to shoot. By this time, the tank machine guns had started blasting. The tracer bullets came close but all missed. The German ran down the back slope of the hill and disappeared. I was relieved; I actually had hoped the bullets would miss this soldier that I had come within seconds of killing. If I had fired that shot, I'm not sure that my strong conscience and sense of ethics would have allowed me the freedom or the right to study medicine.

Bill

Bill was a transfer from an artillery unit that had limited, if any, exposure to infantry combat. He was sent forward to the infantry as part of his punishment for a military infraction. The war was slowly winding down, but there was still active combat. The wounding and killing continued but at a slower pace. On April 9, 1945, we were ordered to attack the small German village of Northeim over a flat, treeless field. The terrain offered no protection from the enemy.

Bill and I were in a small garden cottage on the grounds of an estate waiting for orders to move up. We had been together in several previous attacks, but he had never showed the level of apprehension and nervousness he displayed on this day, in this situation. He released some of his tension by destroying German flags and swords. For some strange reason, I thought of Joyce Kilmer, the author of the poem "Trees," as I watched him. Somewhere I read that just prior to being killed in battle during World War I, Joyce Kilmer had a premonition of death. I think that most of us felt that way prior to an attack. In fact, the waiting period was often worse than the combat. It is at this time that horrible and frightening thoughts race through one's mind. Yet, I was keenly aware of the fact that Bill was more nervous than in previous battles and certainly more nervous than the rest of us.

A short time after noon, we moved into a shallow depression while awaiting the final orders to attack. Bill was on my left as we moved toward the village when he suddenly yelled and fell to the ground. He had been hit by enemy fire. As I examined Bill, I found an entrance wound

91

in the upper-left anterior chest and a larger posterior exit wound at the same level. Both wounds were bleeding and bubbling with respirations. I faced the enemy in a kneeling position and held up the largest white dressing I had for the enemy to see. I then applied a special rubberlike dressing with an adhesive surface protected by a peel-away paper. The wounds required repeated dressing changes in order to maintain a seal. As it happened, a captive German medic had given these dressings to me earlier in the war. This type of cooperation was not unusual. In fact, I had worked with both German physicians and medics while treating the wounded, regardless of uniform. How ironic to need and use German dressings to care for wounds inflicted by German gunfire.

I remained in the kneeling position with Bill's head on my thighs. I was careful not to look in the direction of the enemy, but I discretely scanned the battlefield for the litter-bearers I had seen earlier. Now, they were out of sight. I was torn between leaving Bill to try and find them and staying with him, but Bill had made me promise not to leave him under any circumstance.

Many thoughts raced through my mind. Initially, there was my anger at the litter-bearers, who I believed were hiding in a small-depressed area very close behind us. Then there was guilt for exposing myself, leaving my wife a widow if the enemy were to kill me. I knew that if there were SS troopers (die-hard youths of the Hitlerjugend) in the village, a headshot would be fast and fatal. Perhaps there was a chance that they would shoot to wound only. There is a strange and amazing bond between combat soldiers and medics that make it possible to sacrifice one's own life for a friend or even a perfect stranger.

Bill and I remained in the same position from noon until after darkness fell. Bill was carrying two revolvers. The Luger was under the left shoulder in a modified 45 holster, and the other, a P38, was in the right side of his belt. Bill wanted me to have the revolvers. I cautiously removed them by pulling them down toward the ground. I did not want to be seen by the enemy holding a weapon.

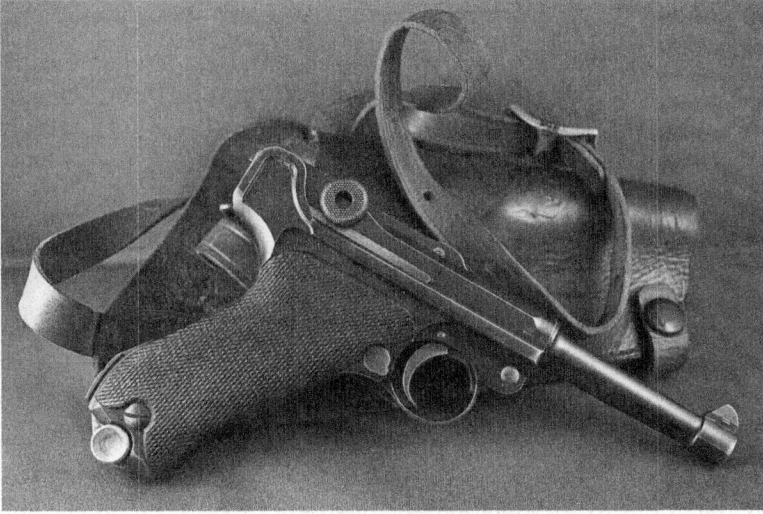

The Luger

After darkness, the litter-bearers came forward. This reinforced my earlier conclusion regarding them. As they carried him back, I held his right hand. He died as he was placed on the Jeep. As I mourned the loss of this soldier in the darkness, I walked aimlessly with no regard for the front line.

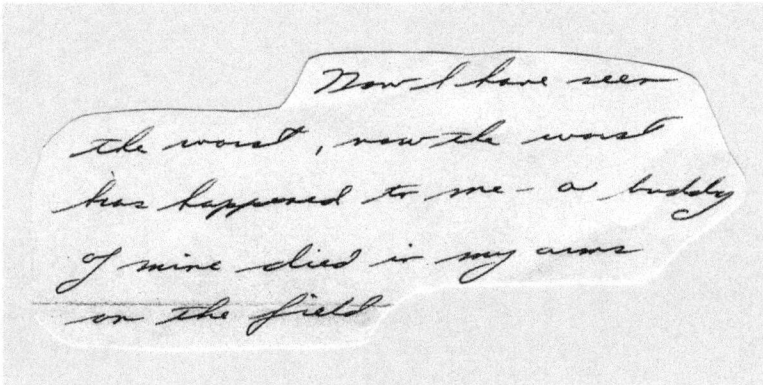

Excerpt from a letter written to my wife.

The following day we took the German village. In a house under a mattress, I found a pair of Zeiss field glasses with the name "Major Bullerdiech" scratched on the front surface. I still have the glasses and often wonder if this major gave the order not to shoot a medic. If so, wherever you are, Major, I thank you.

At the peak of my sorrow and anger, I wrote Bill up for a Silver Star. I hoped that this would square up his military record. I have always thought that those killed in battle deserve a special award in addition to the Purple Heart, perhaps a Gold Star. Likewise, the mothers of those who die in combat are called Gold Star Mothers and deserve this respect.

For my eightieth birthday, my wife and daughter gave me a laptop computer. The first thing I did was to search the Internet for the 104th Infantry Division. As I explored the division's Web site for the very first time, I found a request from Bill's nephew, Captain Jeff, who was looking for information regarding his uncle's death. This request jolted me. Due to his deployment overseas to Iraq and the demands on Captain Jeff, he and I have not been able to meet in person, but we have shared a long telephone conversation. This fateful connection with Bill's nephew rekindled emotions that have never left and will never leave me.

I said what was probably my last goodbye to Bill during an overseas trip in 1999 with the 104th Division Veterans when I visited his grave at the Margraten American Military Cemetery in Holland.

Medics Also Cry

Following the episode with my close friend Bill at Northeim, Germany, I didn't care who saw me cry, because I knew they understood. I remember thinking at the time that perhaps Bill is better off. However, I knew how much he enjoyed life, and I struggled to comprehend his death. It was about that time that the stretcher-bearers were carrying another wounded soldier across the field, and I could hear a lot of yelling and crying. As they set him down, one litter-bearer asked the wounded soldier to please stop yelling and crying. The soldier replied that he was not the one crying, but rather it was one of the other soldiers that was carrying him. That medic had stayed in action too long. He was promptly sent back to a rest area. These same medics had also risked their own lives to pick up a seriously wounded German soldier who lay on the battlefield. I like to think that the Germans would have done the same for us.

Encouraging Signs

As we approached Nordhausen, Germany, on April 10, 1945, we were attacked by gun power from 20 mm ack-ack guns. These guns were fired by women standing outside an open window on one side of a house. Using the building as protection, they fired at us through the open window and across the room toward the opposite side of the building, where we stood outside.

Following this initial contact on the outskirts of Nordhausen, we attacked the Nordhausen concentration camp on the edge of the Hartz Mountains on April 11, 1945. The first part of my regiment attacked while still riding the Third Armored tanks as the rest came through in trucks. It was here that we had our first sight and smell of the German atrocities. No Timberwolf will ever forget the sights and smells of that place. The prisoners were bony skeletons among the dead and dying. The prisoners were used as workers in a factory that was dug deep into the mountainside. This factory manufactured V2 rockets.

Being in a forward tank, we continued through Nordhausen on April 12, 1945, and turned our attack toward the city of Halle on the Saale River, fifty-four miles east of Nordhausen. Therefore, I was not with the medical staff in the tanks who were left to care for these poor souls. Those who were left reported that the townspeople denied knowing anything about the prison camp. Our military immediately ordered the civilians to bury the dead. Certainly one of the most emotional experiences I had during the war was at Nordhausen concentration camp on the edge of the Hartz Mountains. No one will ever forget the sights and smells of that place.

Years later, I often thought I would like to sit in on a current day German history class to see how much of the history being taught is true and accurate. When we returned as civilians in 1999 to tour the battlefields, our guide was a young German who elected public service instead of military duty. The young German took us through Nordhausen, which included a tour of the ovens and a small anteroom next to them. He pointed to the base of what had been a wrought iron hook on the wall of the anteroom. He explained that the so-called doctor of the camp had stuck the ill and dying prisoners on the hook and hung them until they stopped moving, at which time they were transferred to the ovens. After taking this tour and listening to the young German who answered my questions, I would no longer have to wonder what was being taught in modern-day German history classes. This young German knew with clarity the horrifying historic details of World War II. He further explained that when the workers who were prisoners at Nordhausen died or were near death, the other prisoners were ordered to keep on pouring fresh cement on the floor that they were assigned to construct. Many prisoners died in place and were buried as they worked on the cement floor. We were walking on a cement cemetery.

The Wounded Enemy

During the battle for Hill 287 in Stolberg, Germany, I made my initial contact with the wounded enemy. My policy was to treat the more seriously wounded first, regardless of the uniform. I heard some complaints about this, but these fell on deaf ears. In the Battle of the Bulge, I heard there was no respect for the medic's red cross. Personally, I believed that it was all a matter of luck regarding the attitude of the enemy toward medics. The story entitled "Bill," found earlier in this book, gives evidence that the Germans respected medics. Certainly that long afternoon I spent with Bill, as he lay dying in the field allowed the Germans many opportunities to kill a medic; opportunities they chose not to take.

We had just left the Nordhausen concentration camp and were still riding with the Third Armored when I asked the driver to stop so that I could I treat a wounded German by the roadside. The exam revealed a bullet wound through each ankle, apparently made by an automatic weapon. I gave him a shot of morphine in each upper arm. He thanked me profusely, and I patted him on the back. Despite my belief in treating all wounded regardless of the uniform, I often wondered if this German soldier was responsible for any of the atrocities at the concentration camp. I hoped not.

Halle

We entered Halle, Germany, still riding the Third Armored tanks, by crossing over one of the Saale River's few remaining bridges. It was on April 14, 1945, in the midafternoon when we moved into Halle. While the city was known for its large medical center, the community's wealth had come from salt and soft coal mining.

It was here that we began to hear about Count von Luckner, a German who was involved in World War I and ran a gunboat, which was disguised as a pleasure craft. He was a resident of Halle. As I recall, he was a friend of Major General Terry Allen and Lowell Thomas, one of the early radio news reporters. One of the highlights of the battle occurred when Count von Luckner came over to our line under the cover of the flag of truce. He met with Major General Terry Allen and Colonel Kelleher with the objective of making Halle an open city. However, the SS element would not permit a complete surrender, as Halle was a training center for SS troops and the Hitlerjugend. There were always a high percentage of SS troopers in this city, and the fighting in Halle was tough. The battle for Halle would be our last battle and one that we would ultimately win. The battle would last for five days.

Two of my fellow medics were wounded in Halle. Medic Lee Grille was shot in both legs, and medic John Kikich suffered shrapnel wounds. I recall patching up John Kikich. Both of these medics were evacuated from Halle. Around the same time, during the Battle of Halle, the Germans killed one of their own medics for trying to aid a wounded

American soldier. It is my opinion that this soldier died a hero, a good human with big heart and soul.

It was also in Halle that I recall fighting in a small garden house that had been used as a German command post. I walked down a short flight of stairs and found a dead German soldier. I did not touch him for fear of a booby trap. He did not need my help.

In addition to the sounds and sights of human death that constantly surrounded us in Halle, the sound of crying animals that resonated from the depths of the city is forever etched in my memory. The city of Halle had a large zoo. I never did find out if these cries were from hungry or wounded animals. In either case, their pain was severe and left me with a helpless feeling I suspect was similar to what the animals felt.

It's Often Just Plain Luck

In Halle, Germany, there was intense street fighting marked by Panzerfaust sniper and antitank weapon activity. We had just spent some time in the protection of a building when we started to move out. We knew there was a sniper nearby but could not locate him. The rifleman in front of me stepped out of the doorway, when suddenly he spun around and fell back inside the doorway. My examination revealed a bullet hole in the left breast pocket but no signs of blood loss. The bullet had struck and shattered a small Walther revolver that the soldier had been carrying in his breast pocket. The bare skin was intact and showed only redness from the impact. He was almost killed by one German weapon and saved by another. I don't know what happened to the sniper, but that day we all made it unharmed.

During the period we spent on the Roer River, our platoon was making trips across the river and sometimes returned with prisoners. One night a returning squad had just reached our side when they became victims of friendly fire. I heard a BAR go off but stop abruptly as the weapon had jammed. I recall that such a malfunction was not unusual and even characteristic of this weapon. One member of the combat team, a victim of the misfired shots, came up to me with one finger in a bullet hole in his helmet and the other hand holding the bullet he had retrieved after it had stopped rolling around inside his helmet. The bullet never touched him. The soldier normally stuttered,

101

and because of his speech impairment, it seemed like he would never finish telling me his story.

It was at Inden, Germany, where we found several wounded soldiers in a factory. One was lying on his belly eating a K-ration while I was working on the shrapnel wounds between his buttocks and legs. He calmly turned his head and asked if the family jewels were okay. I was happy to inform him that but for only a quarter inch more he would have been a soprano.

It was also at Inden that our sergeant and I were talking in a street just up from the Inde River. A rifleman yelled from a second story for us to get out of "88 alley," which was under heavy fire from 88 mm shelling. Just then, a shell hit the inside of the window frame, killing the rifleman who had just warned us.

It wasn't always all fighting. There were times when my duties as a medic were not needed. During lulls in city fighting and whenever it was practical, I would set up a darkroom to develop pictures. The officers in charge assigned a Jeep and a driver to accompany me across the river to restock our photo supplies at the Agfa plant. We were in a hurry because we could hear the horse-drawn wagons of the Russians approaching in the distance. I opened a door on one of those upper floors and, unaware, started to step into open space. The soldier behind me grabbed me around the neck, and we fell backward onto the floor. He had recognized the empty elevator shaft that I was about to inadvertently step into. His quick action prevented a serious accident or even my death. Wherever you are, old friend, thank you again. The enemy is not always to blame for all wartime deaths. Often it's just plain bad luck.

One night we were in a factory along the Inden River across from Inden, Germany, preparing to move out. At the time, we were carrying an extra lieutenant. During a shelling from those "screaming meemies," this young lieutenant asked me if I ever got used to combat. I gave him my opinion that perhaps I did to some degree. It isn't that I got used to it but rather learned to live with the reality of it. A soldier's ability or caution did not guarantee his safety. Often a soldier's fate was just plain luck. The fear and sadness, however, never leaves the soldier.

On Thanksgiving, during active combat, the cooks brought us a hot dinner on the front line. A shell hit the room we were in, killing one of the cooks. No one else was hit. We had all spent a fair amount of time up at the front with the exception of the cooks. It seemed ironic that a cook would be the one to go. When I think about this dinner and the death of this noncombatant cook, I once again have to wonder if perhaps it's not just plain luck, but rather the will of a higher power.

The Old Sergeant Syndrome

I vividly remember a short blond American tanker sergeant who suddenly started crying during battle. I pulled him into a storefront for protection and preformed a negative exam. Closer questioning revealed that in a previous battle his best friend had both legs blown off at the knee level and had then run on the stumps before suddenly falling over dead. The present fighting brought this dramatic and vivid memory back to this young tanker sergeant, virtually paralyzing him.

I sent the tanker sergeant back from the front line and hoped that he would not be sent up again. This soldier had reached the psychological breaking point. I doubted if he could be rehabilitated. His was an example of "the old sergeant syndrome"—that is, one who has an outstanding combat record and often is decorated but has reached the breaking point and cannot be salvaged to return to combat.

As I was dragging the sergeant into a relatively safe area, I noticed a tall soldier in the alley to my left pulling a German soldier by his feet. Blood was pouring from the German's head and neck region. I had seen this fellow soldier in action before. His intention was not one of mercy but rather looting. The day before I had caught him pulling a wedding ring off a German girl's finger, and I had given him a tongue-lashing. He returned the ring and apologized. I did not have much rank but was respected because the troops never knew when my services would be needed.

The Highest VD Rate

One of our heavy weapons platoons had the highest VD (venereal disease) rate in the division and possibly the entire ETO (European Theater of Operations). A soldier, who said he thought a German girl had exposed him to VD, awakened me one night. I got dressed and called a Jeep driver to take him to the aid station for a prophylactic treatment. The next morning I asked the soldier if there were any problems. He then told me that he had discovered that he really did not need the prophylactic treatment the previous night, because he was told that another German girl was simply jealous and had fabricated the venereal disease story. Believing this young girl's story, the soldier went back and spent the rest of the night with the same girl. No wonder this group had the highest rate of infection. Some people never learn.

Nature's Way

I cannot recall the name of the village, but there was intense fighting at the time. We ducked into an alley for some protection and found two German couples engaged in some intense lovemaking. With the amount of shelling and small arms fire all around us, it seemed surreal that the acts of love and violence were occurring simultaneously. Then I started to think about what they were doing and realized that it was certainly more natural than the battle. I also thought about how nature has a way of maintaining a balance. Their activity might lead to new birth, whereas ours would certainly lead to death. Perhaps by the end of the day some obscure balance in nature would be struck as a result of these drastically opposing acts.

Strange Priorities

During combat in Germany, an incident happened that was perplexing. We were on the outskirts of a village where a tank battle was being fought. Our objective was to stay out of the way of any stray shells, as we were not really involved in that particular fighting. We noticed that on the side of a mountain there were some horizontal mine shafts, so we stepped in there to keep out of trouble. We had only been there a short time when a German lady came rushing out of the little village. She was very upset. We asked why, and she told us she was afraid that her laundry, which she had just put out on the line, might get damaged or dirty. She apparently never even considered that she might be in danger from the shelling. Some people have strange priorities or perhaps the protective ability to deny reality.

Souvenirs Alive with Memories

When we were fighting in Cologne, some of the boys found a microscope in a bombed laboratory along the Rhine. They brought it to me and said, "Perhaps you can use this when you go to medical school, Doc." As it turned out, owning your own microscope was one of the prerequisites for Tufts Medical School. The microscope that I brought home from Germany is the same microscope that I use in my office today. It often brings back many memories when I use it.

One day in Halle, I stumbled across a movie projector. I was looking at it outside a bombed brick building when a lieutenant from my home state came along and said, "I'll take that, Coe." At that point I replied, "What you mean is you'll take that because you outrank me." He said, "Yes," so I responded, "Well, why don't we split it?" I reached over, took the lens, smashed it against the stonewall, and said, "Lieutenant, you can have the other half. I don't want my half."

Night Attack

I recall a night attack in Germany when we were approaching an old castle-like structure. American and German soldiers shared a dislike for night fighting. The terrain was rough under foot; we fell into holes, and we got tangled in heavy vines and wire fences. I offered my unskilled talent in compass reading, which was of little help. Ultimately, upon reaching the building, we found several wounded Germans and a female physician. We gave them what help we could in the way of medical attention before moving on. If this place had been properly defended, I doubt any of us would have survived.

An Emotional Experience

When the war ended, we were in a small German village near the Mulde River. The pressure of combat pushed families away from the front line and made it necessary for them to move in together. My platoon was staying at a house that had two women, each of whom had a daughter. Our boys left the girls alone. One of the girls was flirting with our sergeant, who was a shy person. He remained respectful.

We had been very good to our German hosts, which included giving them a share of the double portions in our mess kits. We slept on the floor and left the beds for them. There were two dogs in the house; one was a German police dog, the other a dachshund. The latter found his way to me during the night and slept with me. After the war, one of the first things I did was to get a dachshund.

The war had been over for one week, and suddenly we were alerted to help out a platoon that was pinned down by a fanatical SS group. I started to search for my aid pouches and turned to see the owner of the house (one of the two women) standing in the middle of the living room holding my aid pouches tightly and crying. I asked her why she was crying. Between sobs she told me that she was afraid that one of us would be killed or wounded. This human emotion exemplified by this German woman for American soldiers is another example of the stupidity of war. At the last minute, we were called off. We were all relieved, including the German lady who had seemed more concerned about us than we were. We were friends and no longer enemies.

Medic Fred Hughes, our German Hostess and her Daughter,
Medic Israel Jaffe

A Tragic Ending

At the end of April 1945, American and Russian soldiers were in contact with each other on the Mulde and Elbe Rivers. May 4, 1945, marked the significant end of 195 consecutive days of frontline combat. We had never been pulled off the front lines. On May 7, 1945, we received the official announcement that the war in Europe was over.

Russian Soldiers

On June 11, 1945, we moved by rail in 40 and 8s on to Le Havre, France. This was the start of our long-awaited trip home, the moment every soldier yearned for, no matter which side of the war he was on.

It was the same way we traveled when we began the war. On June 19, 1945, we arrived in Le Havre and found the Lucky Strike Tent Camp, where we stayed until we boarded the ship for home.

Shipping out at Le Havre, France

On July 2, 1945, we boarded the *MS Ericsson* bound for the United States of America and arrived at Staten Island, New York, on July 11, 1945. One tragedy took place on the trip back home. There were many souvenirs carried on board by the soldiers, and these included weapons. It was our understanding that the firing pins had been removed from all weapons. One of our soldiers was cleaning and inspecting his souvenir German revolver when it accidentally fired and killed one of his fellow roommates. As soldiers and medics, we believed and hoped that death had been left behind us. I would learn in civilian life that the memory and reality of death and war would forever remain a part of all our lives, never to be fully left behind.

Oddly enough, I missed the vision of sailing into New York harbor because I was taking a freshwater shower. After a year of inadequate bathing, done mostly from a helmet full of water, I was determined to get a shower. Although it took me the entire transatlantic crossing to successfully barter with a sailor for a cold but freshwater shower, I ultimately succeeded. This was likely to be the most expensive and most memorable shower of my life.

A typical bath

Upon arrival in Staten Island, we were given a thirty-day recuperation furlough. While war in the European Theater had ended, war in the Pacific Theater remained active. Following these thirty days of rest, we were to report for further training in order to be deployed once again. Returning home was a strange feeling. Being among my family was different. They had not changed, but I had. I spent my furlough back home with my wife and family in Durham, Connecticut. As active servicemen, we remained in military uniform during our furlough.

During this recuperation furlough, I was visiting my mother and sitting casually on the kitchen counter. Suddenly, a nearby firecracker exploded outside the kitchen window. I went flying off the counter, landing face down on the kitchen floor, flat on my chest and abdomen. This conditioned reflex embarrassed me in front of my family, but they all seemed to understand. This was a well-ingrained and conditioned reflex, which had helped to keep me alive. It was an instinct of survival. A rapid response was often the difference between life and death.

During this leave, my wife Eleanor and I were in a theater in Middletown, Connecticut, when it was suddenly flashed on the screen that Japan had surrendered. I felt like I had been pardoned from a death sentence. I would not have to return to combat. Great joy was followed by sadness when I thought of those who did not return, including General Rose, commander of the Third Armored who was born right there in Middletown and had been killed in action. Just then, while I was deep in my thoughts, the lady sitting to the left of my wife reached over, tapped me on the arm, and said, "Thank you." These were the kindest words since this whole mess started. I will always remember them.

Going Home

Although Japan had surrendered, the official end of the war had not been 100 percent secured; thus, we reassembled at Camp San Luis Obispo, California, after our thirty-day leave. During this time, we were still scheduled for training in Pacific Theater combat, where we would be sent if no official end to the war came. After the official VJ Day (Victory in Japan) on September 2, 1945, discharge was an official reality. The order of a soldier's discharge was based on a point system, which depended on length and type of service in addition to any awards one might have received during combat service. Following VJ Day, we eagerly began adding up our points, knowing that the higher the number of points we had, the sooner we would be discharged. On November 8, 1945, I was discharged from San Luis Obispo. My wife and my Aunt Marion drove from the east coast to pick me up. As we drove back east toward home, I was keenly aware that I was at that very moment teetering between two very different chapters of my life. Each day of the next chapter of my life would be influenced by the experiences of war. As a young man, I could not have imagined to what degree the war would influence my life and form the person I am today.

Many of the friendships made with the 104th Timberwolf Division last a lifetime; mine certainly have. There is a special bond between those who have experienced combat together. It is a bond that is of equal strength today and holds even greater meaning with the passing of time.

Looking forward ...

Returning to the Battlefields

In the spring of 1999, a group of us made a return trip to the battlefields. This was one of several trips that had been made by the 104th Division Veterans, but the first trip for my wife and me.

During this trip, we visited the Henri-Chapelle American Cemetery in Belgium and the Margraten American Military Cemetery in the Netherlands. I was able to locate some of the graves of soldiers I knew and took care of. For a brief time, while standing at their gravesites, I could see them once again as living people. After all, isn't this one of the reasons why we visit the burial sites of our friends and relatives? To stand among these marble crosses where our comrades still remain in military formation is overwhelming. It is a perpetual military formation of the dead. I often think of the fact that these soldiers never came home like the rest of us.

In addition to remembering the dead, I felt a strong need to come face to face with the former enemy. My desire was satisfied during this trip to Germany. We had the Timberwolf patch on our caps when an English-speaking German male came up to us and said, "Hey, you guys; the last time I saw you I was shooting 'ack-ack' [antiaircraft artillery frequently used against ground troops] at you." We told him that we were glad he missed some of us. We shook hands, hugged each other, and even joked a bit. I had expected and hoped for this kind of meeting.

We toured the prison were Hitler killed his former officials who had plotted against him. He killed them by hanging them with piano wire. While visiting this German jail, we met another former German soldier. My wife was talking with the former soldier and his wife when he indicated that we had once been neighbors. While I was in combat training at Camp Carson in Colorado Springs, Colorado, he had been a POW there. How strange to realize that we had been in the same camp but for a different purpose. On another occasion, I met their son, Matthias J. Maurer, who had written a book about our division titled *Our Way to Halle*. He had attended many of our division reunions and was also instrumental in the placement of a memorial plaque for our Timberwolf Division in his hometown of Halle, Germany. The plaque had been placed to commemorate and specifically remember the successful negotiations that saved Halle from total destruction. Count von Luckner, the German who had tried to negotiate the liberation of Halle with General Terry Allen, was involved in these negotiations. Matthias is and deserves to be an honorary Timberwolf for securing the history of our division and its part in making peace.

Afterword

My experiences during the war may be recalled spontaneously by sounds, sights, or odors. The state of war represents a complete breakdown in civilization. I observed that there is a release of early man's survival instinct, which includes killing as many of your fellow men that are classified as the enemy as is possible. At another time, under different circumstances, these same people may have been close friends. Wild animals that kill for hunger have a better reason to kill than does man.

War is like many of life's violent experiences, except that these experiences happen in greater numbers and usually to those of a young age. I have often thought of combat as a combination of severe and tragic accidents, which would include fire, lightning strikes, floods, and all the natural disasters. Man has engaged in conflict since the beginning of time, so perhaps, on second thought, war, too, should be thought of as a natural disaster.

Resources

Books

Astor, Gerald. *Terrible Terry Allen: The Soldier's General*. New York: The Ballantine Books, 2003.

Barber, Frederick A. *The Horror Of It: Camera Records Of War's Gruesome Glories*. New York: Association Press, 1932.

Bishop, Chris. *The Encyclopedia of Weapons of World War II*. New York: Metrobooks, 2002.

Cooper, Belton Y. *Death Traps*. California: Presidio Press, Inc., 1998.

Hoegh, Leo A., and Howard J. Doyle. *Timberwolf Tracks: The History of The 104th Infantry Division 1942-1945*. Washington: Infantry Journal Press, Inc., 1946.

Maurer, Matthias J. *Our Way to Halle: A Count of the 104th Combat Division*. Germany: Beilage zum Buch, 1999.

Yeide, Harry. *The Longest Battle*. Minneapolis: Zenith Press, 2005.

Magazine, Pamphlet, and Newspaper Articles

Allen, Major General Terry. 1945. "The Trail of the Timberwolves." California: 104th Infantry Division.

Clyma, Carleton B. "Connecticut Men of the 104th Division." *Servicemen's Commemorative Booklet* Volume I, Number 4, July 1945.

Combat History 414th Infantry Regiment 104th Infantry Division Monthly Operation Reports 414th Infantry Regiment, 104th Infantry Division October 1944–April 1945, submitted by the commander.

Multiple Articles: Middletown Press 1943–1945

Multiple Articles: New Haven Register 1943–1945

Timberwolves: The Story of the 104th Infantry Division (This booklet is one of the series of G.I. Stories) Paris: Stars & Stripes Publishers 1944-1945

The Timberwolf Howl, post World War II–current

CPSIA information can be obtained
at www.ICGtesting.com
Printed in the USA
BVOW03*0125161117
500566BV00006B/16/P